Introduction to Our New NE__ _____

The Science Coordination Group was set up with the aim of producing specialised revision material for National Curriculum Science. Following popular demand we have taken our very successful Revision Guides for GCSE double science and from them produced a number of syllabus-specific versions for the NEAB and SEG double science syllabuses.

All of our Revision Guides exhibit several crucial features which set them apart from the rest:

1) Careful and Complete Explanations

Unlike other revision guides, we do not restrict ourselves to a brief outline of the bare essentials. Instead we work hard to give complete, concise and carefully written details on each topic.

2) Deliberate Use of Humour and Colourful Language

We consider the humour to be an essential part of our Revision Guides. It is there to keep the reader interested and entertained, and we are certain that it greatly assists their learning.
(It is not however expected to win us any awards...)

3) Carefully Matched to the NEAB Coordinated Syllabus, and more...

We have taken great care to ensure that this book follows the exact detail of the NEAB double award coordinated syllabus.
Once again however we feel that merely illustrating the syllabus is an inadequate approach. We have therefore done rather more than simply list the basic syllabus details and add pictures. Instead we have endeavoured to include all the relevant explanation which appears to us to be necessary. The result is a full 96 pages giving a clear explanation of the whole syllabus content. We hope you will appreciate the amount of time and care which has gone into this.

> **Higher** This book is suitable for both Higher and Foundation Tier candidates.
> The material which is required only for Higher Tier is clearly indicated in blue boxes like this. **Higher**
> In addition, the Higher Tier questions in the Revision Summaries are printed in blue.

And Keep Learning the Basic Facts...

Throughout these books there is constant emphasis on the inescapable need to *__keep learning the basic facts__*. This simple message is hammered home without compromise and without remorse, and whilst this traditionally brutal philosophy may not be quite in line with some other approaches to education, we still rather like it. But only because it works.

Contents

Section One — Life Processes & Cell Activity

(1.1) Basic Principles
- Life and Cells 1
- Specialised Cells 2
- Tissues and Organs 3
- Exchange Surfaces 4

(1.2) Transport Across Boundaries
- Diffusion 5
- Diffusion Through Membranes 6
- Osmosis 7
- Active Uptake 8
- Revision Summary For Section One 9

Section Two — Humans as Organisms

(2.1) Nutrition
- The Digestive System 10
- Digestive Enzymes 11
- The Human Diet 12

(2.2) Circulation
- The Circulatory System 13
- The Heart 14
- The Pumping Cycle 15
- Blood Vessels 16
- Blood 17

(2.3) Breathing
- Lungs and Breathing 18
- Alveoli, Cells and Diffusion 19

(2.4) Respiration
- Respiration 20

(2.5) The Nervous System
- The Eye 21
- The Nervous System 22
- Neurones and Reflexes 23

(2.6) Hormones
- Hormones 24
- Insulin and Diabetes 25
- Female Menstrual Cycle 26
- Menstrual Cycle Hormones 27

(2.7) Homeostasis
- Homeostasis 28
- Skin and Temperature 29
- Kidneys 30
- Ultrafiltration and ADH 31

(2.8) Disease
- Causes of Disease 32
- Disease in Humans 33
- Fighting Disease 34
- Immunisation 35

(2.9) Drugs
- Drugs 36
- Revision Summary for Section Two 37

Section Three — Green Plants as Organisms

(3.1) Plant Nutrition
- Basic Plant Structure 39
- Photosynthesis 40
- The Rate of Photosynthesis 41
- How Plants Use The Glucose 42
- Minerals For Healthy Growth 43

(3.2) Plant Hormones
- Growth Hormones in Plants 44
- Commercial Use of Hormones 45

(3.3) Transport and Water Relations
- The Transpiration Stream 46
- The Cells' Role in Transpiration 47
- Transport Systems in Plants 48
- Revision Summary For Section Three 49

(Syllabus Reference)

Section Four — Variation, Inheritance & Evolution

- (4.1) Variation — Variation in Plants and Animals — 50
- (4.2) Genetics and DNA — Genetics: Too Many Fancy Words — 52
- " " " — Genes, Chromosomes and DNA — 53
- (1.3) Cell Division — Ordinary Cell Division: Mitosis — 54
- " " — DNA Replication in Mitosis — 55
- " " — Gamete Production: Meiosis — 56
- (4.2) Genetics and DNA — Fertilisation: Meeting of Gametes — 57
- " " " — Mutations — 58
- " " " — X & Y Chromosomes — 59
- " " " — Breeding Terminology — 60
- " " " — Monohybrid Crosses: Hamsters — 61
- " " " — Cystic Fibrosis — 62
- " " " — Other Genetic Diseases — 63
- (4.3) Controlling Inheritance — Selective Breeding — 64
- " " — Cloning — 66
- " " — Cloned Plants — 67
- " " — Genetic Engineering — 68
- (4.4) Evolution — Evolution — 69
- " — Fossils — 70
- " — Natural Selection — 72
- " — Revision Summary for Section Four — 74

Section Five — Living Things in Their Environment

- (5.1) Adaptation and Competition — Population Size & Distribution — 75
- " " " — Adapt and Survive — 76
- " " " — Predators and Prey — 77
- (5.2) Human Impact on the Environment — There's Too Many People — 78
- " " " " " — Acid Rain — 79
- " " " " " — Problems Caused By Farming — 80
- " " " " " — The Greenhouse Effect — 81
- (5.3) Energy and Nutrient Transfer — Food Webs — 82
- " " " " — Making Holes in Food Webs — 83
- " " " " — Pyramids Of Number & Biomass — 84
- " " " " — Energy Transfer & Efficient Food — 85
- (5.4) Nutrient Cycles — Decomposition & the Carbon Cycle — 86
- " " — The Nitrogen Cycle — 87
- " " — Revision Summary for Section Five — 88

Index — 89

(Syllabus Reference)

Published by Coordination Group Publications
Typesetting and Layout by The Science Coordination Group
Illustrations by: Sandy Gardner, e-mail: zimkit@aol.com

Consultant Editor: Paddy Gannon BSc MA

Text, design, layout and illustrations © Richard Parsons 1997, 1998.   All rights reserved.
With thanks to CorelDRAW for providing one or two jolly bits of clipart.

Printed by Hindson Print, Newcastle upon Tyne.

LIFE PROCESSES & CELL ACTIVITY

Life and Cells — Basic Principles

The Seven Life Processes which show you're alive

There are seven things they call "LIFE PROCESSES", — things that all plants and animals do.
You should learn all seven well enough to write them down from memory.
Use the little jollyism "MRS NERG" to remind you of the first letter of each word.

M — Movement	Being able to move parts of the body.
R — Reproduction	Producing offspring.
S — Sensitivity	Responding to the outside world.
N — Nutrition	Getting food in where it's needed.
E — Excretion	Getting rid of waste products.
R — Respiration	Turning food into energy.
G — Growth	Getting to adult size.

(If you think about it, this list describes the entire life of a sheep — and a frighteningly large chunk of yours too.)

Plant Cells and Animal Cells Have Their Differences

You need to be able to draw these two cells WITH ALL THE DETAILS for each.

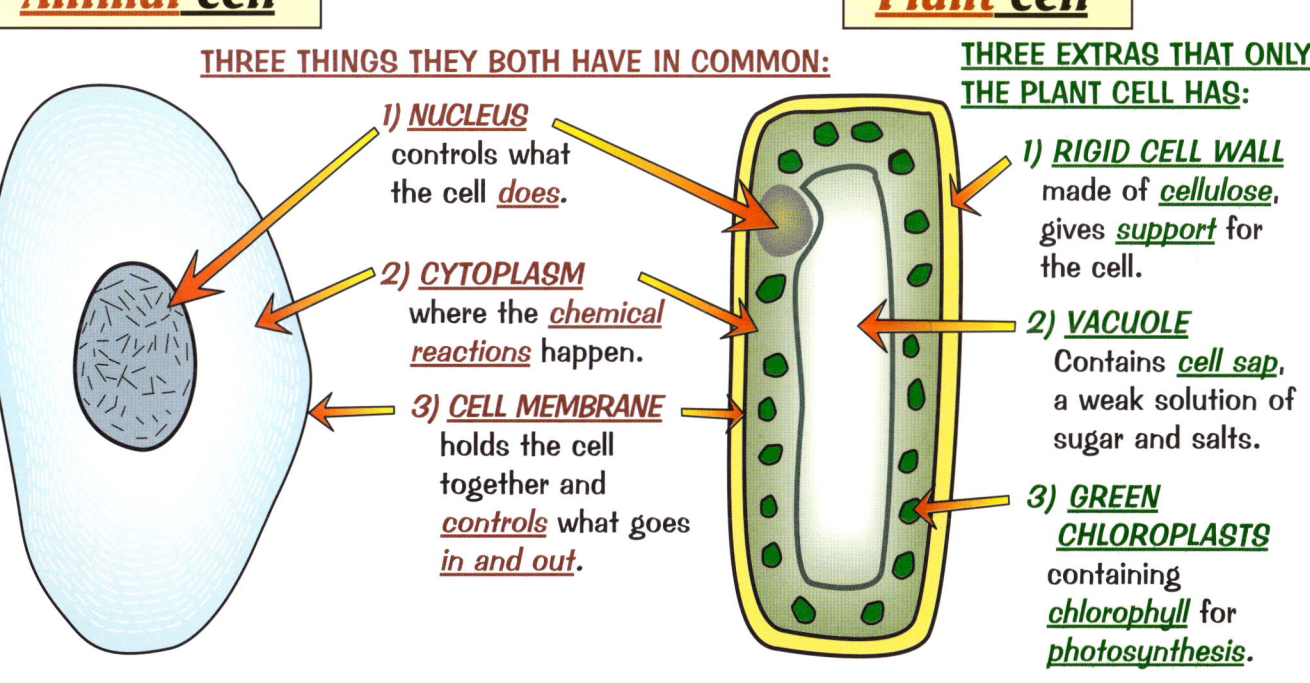

Animal Cell

Plant Cell

THREE THINGS THEY BOTH HAVE IN COMMON:

1) **NUCLEUS** controls what the cell does.
2) **CYTOPLASM** where the chemical reactions happen.
3) **CELL MEMBRANE** holds the cell together and controls what goes in and out.

THREE EXTRAS THAT ONLY THE PLANT CELL HAS:

1) **RIGID CELL WALL** made of cellulose, gives support for the cell.
2) **VACUOLE** Contains cell sap, a weak solution of sugar and salts.
3) **GREEN CHLOROPLASTS** containing chlorophyll for photosynthesis.

Have you learnt it? — let's see, shall we...

Right then, when you're ready, when you think you've learnt it, cover the page and answer these:
1) What are the seven life processes, and what's the little jolly for remembering them?
2) Draw an animal cell and a plant cell and put all the labels on them.
3) What three things do plant and animal cells have in common?
4) What are the three differences between them?

Specialised Cells

Basic Principles

Most cells are *SPECIALISED* for a specific job, and in the Exam you'll probably have to explain why the cell they've shown you is so good at its job. It's a lot easier if you've *already learnt them*!

1) Palisade Leaf Cells are Designed for Photosynthesis

1) Packed with *chloroplasts* for *photosynthesis*.
2) *Tall* shape means a lot of *surface area* exposed down the side for *absorbing CO_2* from the air in the leaf.
3) Tall shape also means a good chance of *light* hitting a *chloroplast* before it reaches the bottom of the cell.

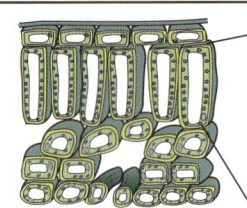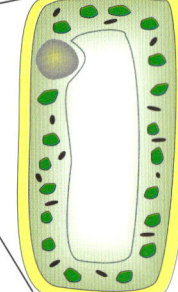

2) Guard Cells are Designed to Open and Close

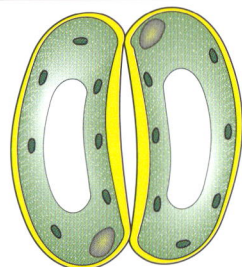

1) Special *kidney shape* which *opens* and *closes* the stomata (a single pore is a stoma) as the cells go *turgid* or *flaccid*.
2) *Thin* outer walls and *thickened* inner walls make this opening and closing function work properly.
3) They're also *sensitive to light* and *close at night* to conserve water without losing out on photosynthesis.

3) Red blood cells are Designed to Carry Oxygen

1) *Doughnut* shaped to allow maximum oxygen absorption by the *haemoglobin* they contain. The function is similar to the palisade cells above. They are *doughnut* shaped rather than *tall* to allow smooth passage through the *capillaries*.
2) They are so packed with *haemoglobin* that they have no room for a *nucleus*.

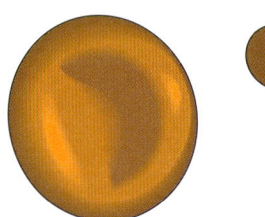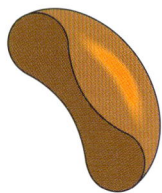

4) Sperm and egg cells are specialised for Reproduction

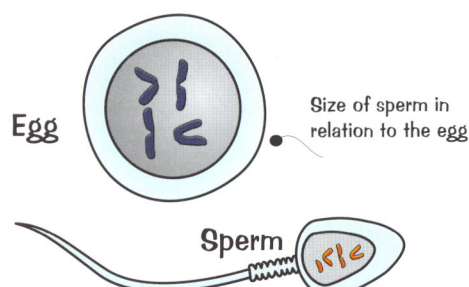

Egg

Size of sperm in relation to the egg

Sperm

1) The *egg* cell has huge food reserves to provide nutrition for the developing embryo.
2) When a *sperm* fuses with the egg, the egg's *membrane* instantly changes to prevent any more sperm getting in.
3) A long *tail* gives the sperm the *mobility* needed for its long journey to find the egg.
4) The sperm also has a *short life-span* so only the fittest survive the race to the egg.

5) Five Other Important Examples:

There are five other important examples of specialised cells: *Root Hair cells* (P. 8), *Phloem cells* (P. 48), *Xylem cells* (P. 3), *White blood cells* (P. 17) and *Nerve cells* (P. 23). Look them up and see how they're specialised.

OK, let's see what you know..

When you think you've **LEARNT** everything on this page, *cover it up*. Now sketch the nine specialised cells mentioned on this page and point out their special features.

Tissues and Organs

Basic Principles

They like asking this in Exams, so learn the sequence:

> A group of **SIMILAR CELLS** is called a **TISSUE**.
> A group of **DIFFERENT TISSUES** form an **ORGAN**.
> A **GROUP OF ORGANS** working together form an **ORGAN SYSTEM**,
> or even **A WHOLE ORGANISM**.

This can apply to animals as well as plants, of course.

An Exciting Plant Example

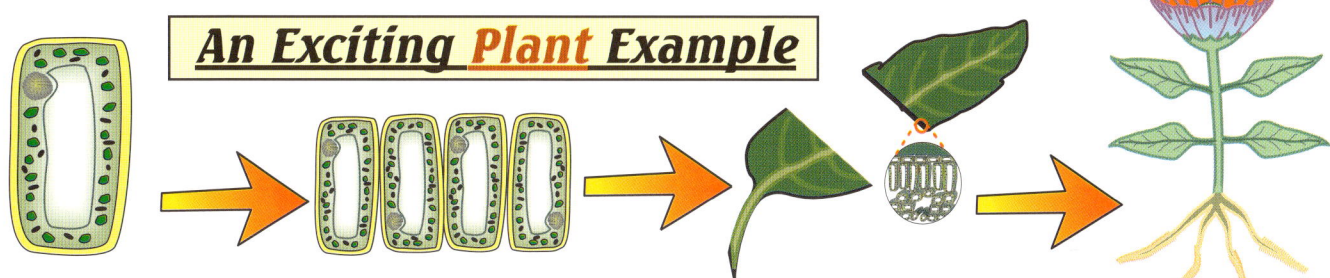

Palisade **CELLS**... ...make up palisade **TISSUE**... ...which, with other tissues make up a leaf (an **ORGAN**)... ...and leaves and other organs make up a full plant (an **ORGANISM**).

Specialised Animal Tissue — Muscular and Glandular

You can find examples of specialised _tissue_ all over the place. In this example, _muscle_ and _glandular_ tissue join forces to make the small intestine which is part of the digestive _organ system_.

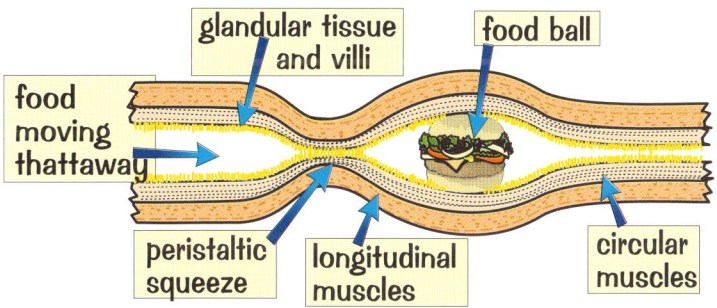

There's _muscular tissue_ all the way down the digestive system. All muscle tissue has the _ability to contract_ which in this case _squeezes the food along_.

The _inside layer_ is _glandular tissue_ which secretes the various _digestive enzymes_, as well as a _protective mucus_.

Specialised Plant Tissue — Xylem

1) Xylem tissue forms a _xylem tube_ made up of _dead cells_ joined end to end with _no end walls_ between them.

2) The side walls are _strong and stiff_ to give the plant _support_.

3) The xylem tubes carry _water and minerals_ from the _roots_ up to the _leaves_ in the transpiration stream.

(You'll learn more about the phloem tubes in section three — bet you can't wait.)

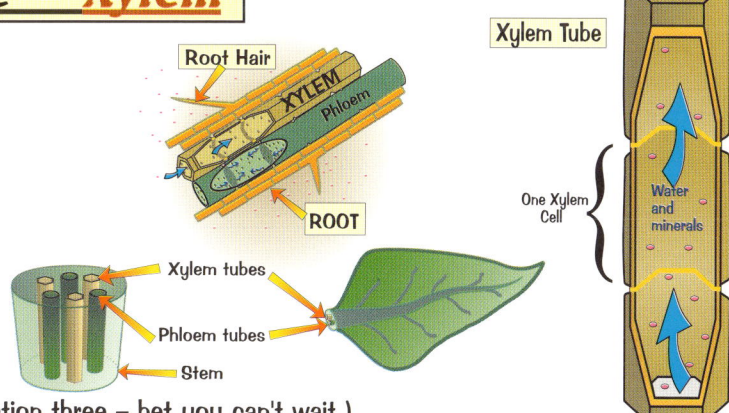

So What have you LEARNED?

Make sure that you learn the sequence from cells to organ-systems and the example given on this page. Learn all four of the specialised organs mentioned and _practise drawing and labelling_ them from memory. It's really important to learn exactly _how and why_ each of the organs is specialised.

SECTION ONE — LIFE PROCESSES & CELL ACTIVITY   NEAB Syllabus

Exchange Surfaces

Basic Principles

Everything in plants and animals is specialised. This includes the cells, the tissues, organs, organ-systems and indeed whole organisms. The organ-systems on this page are specialised to exchange materials — learn them.

1) The Villi Provide a Really Really Big Surface Area

The inside of the _small intestine_ is covered in _millions and millions_ of these tiny little projections called _VILLI_.

They _increase_ the _surface area_ in a big way so that digested food is _absorbed_ much more quickly into the _blood_.

Notice they have a _very thin_ layer of cells and a very good _blood supply_ to assist _quick absorption_.

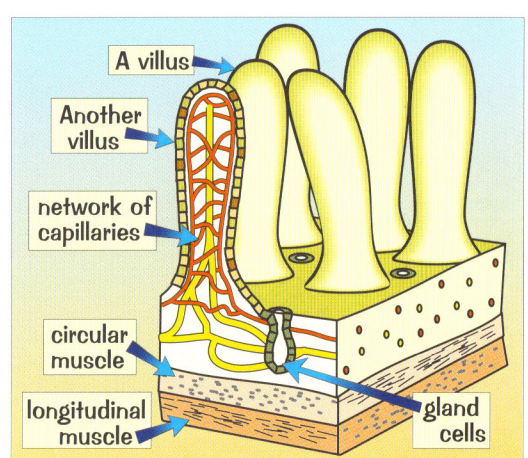

2) Plants use Big Surface Areas at the Roots and Leaves

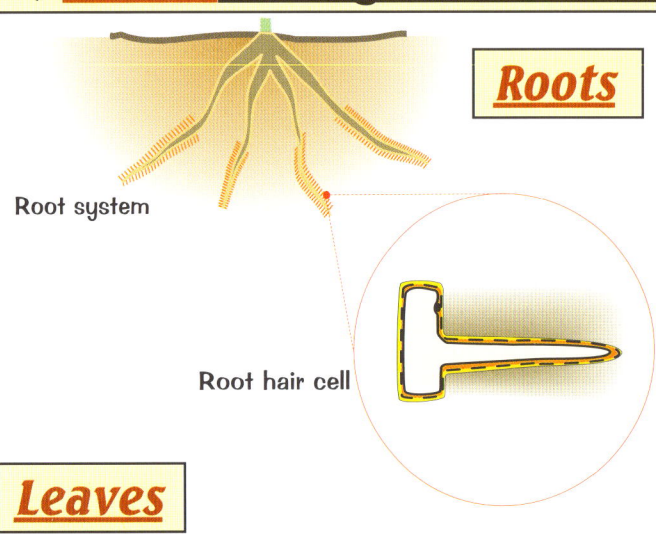

Root system

Root hair cell

Roots

A large root network and the _root hair cells_ help produce a large surface area at the bottom of the plant. This surface area is used to obtain _water_ and _minerals_ from the soil (P. 8).

Leaves

A _flattened shape_ and _internal air spaces_ give leaves a huge surface area.
You can see how the plant utilises this surface area for _diffusion_ (P. 5) and _photosynthesis_ (P. 40).

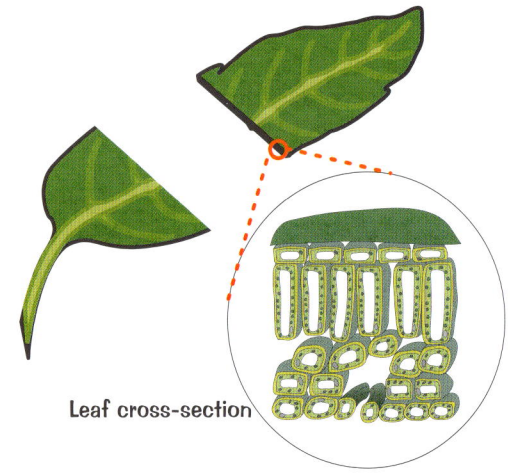

Leaf cross-section

3) Lungs are the Other Important Example

Another area where a large surface area is of great importance is in the _lungs_ where specialised organs called _alveoli_ perform gaseous exchange. See P. 6 and P. 19 for some groovy pictures.

Leaf nothing to chance — get organised...

A real clever trick for learning lots of information is to get an overall image in your head of what each page looks like. It can really help you to remember all the little details. Try it with this page. _Learn_ the three diagrams, with all their little labels. Then _cover the page_ and try and _picture the whole thing_ in your head. Then try and _scribble it all down_. It takes practice but you _can_ do it.

Diffusion

Transport Across Boundaries

Don't be put off by the fancy word

"Diffusion" is really simple. It's just the _gradual movement of particles_ from places where there are _lots of them_ to places where there are _less of them_. That's all it is — IT'S JUST THE NATURAL TENDENCY FOR STUFF TO SPREAD OUT.

Unfortunately you also have to LEARN the fancy way of saying the same thing, which is this:

DIFFUSION is the MOVEMENT OF PARTICLES from an area of HIGH CONCENTRATION to an area of LOW CONCENTRATION

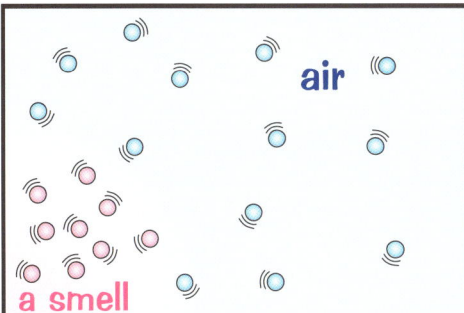

Diffusion of Gases in Leaves is vital for Photosynthesis

The _simplest type_ of diffusion is where _different gases diffuse through each other_, like when a weird smell spreads out through the air in a room. Diffusion of gases also happens in _leaves_ and they'll very likely put it in your Exam. _So learn it now_:

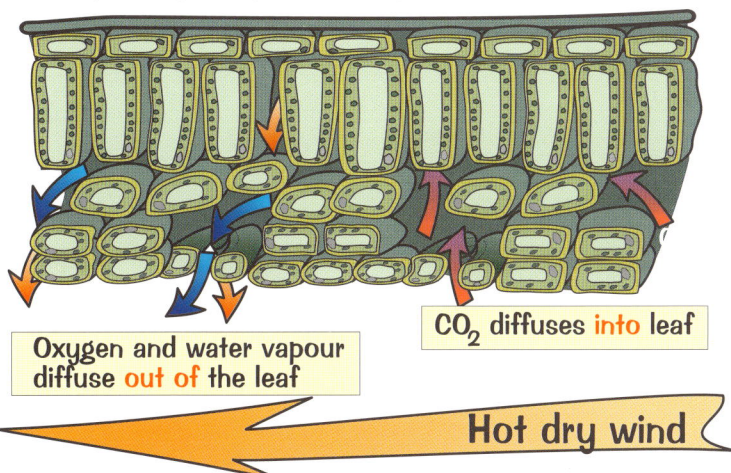

For PHOTOSYNTHESIS to happen, carbon dioxide gas has to get _inside the leaves_.

It does this by DIFFUSION through the biddy little holes under the leaf called stomata. At the same time water vapour and oxygen diffuse _out_ through the same biddy little holes.

The water vapour escapes by _diffusion_ because there's a lot of it _inside_ the leaf and less of it in the air _outside_. This diffusion causes TRANSPIRATION and it goes _quicker_ when the air around the leaf is kept DRY — i.e. transpiration is quickest in HOT, DRY, WINDY CONDITIONS — and don't you forget it!

So, how much do you know about diffusion?

Yeah sure it's a pretty book but actually the big idea is to _learn_ all the stuff that's in it.
So learn this page until you can answer these questions _without having to look back_:

1) Write down the fancy definition for diffusion, and then say what it means in your own words.
2) Draw the cross-section of the leaf with arrows to show which way the three gases diffuse.
3) What weather conditions make the diffusion of water vapour out of the leaf go fastest?

SECTION ONE — LIFE PROCESSES & CELL ACTIVITY   NEAB SYLLABUS

Diffusion Through Membranes

Transport Across Boundaries

Cell membranes are kind of clever...

They're kind of clever because they hold everything *inside* the cell, BUT, they let stuff *in and out* as well. Only very *small molecules* can diffuse through cell membranes though — things like *sugar*, *water* or *ions*.

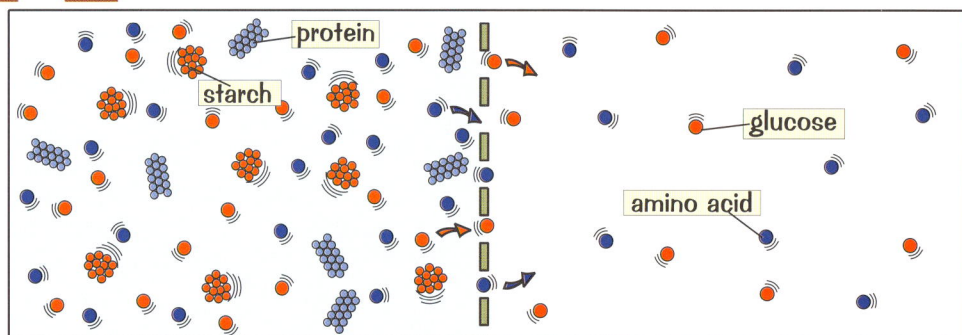

1) Notice that BIG MOLECULES like STARCH or PROTEINS can't diffuse through cell membranes — they could quite cheerfully ask you exactly that in the Exam.
2) Just like with diffusion in air, particles flow through the cell membrane from where there's a HIGH CONCENTRATION (a lot of them) to where there's a LOW CONCENTRATION (not such a lot of them).
3) The RATE OF DIFFUSION is directly affected by the concentration gradient — "The greater the difference in concentration the faster the rate of diffusion". Now don't you forget that.

Gas Exchange in the Lungs

The lungs contain millions and millions of little air sacs called ALVEOLI (see diagram opposite) which are specialised to maximise the diffusion of oxygen and CO_2. The ALVEOLI are an ideal EXCHANGE SURFACE. They have:

1) An ENORMOUS SURFACE AREA (about 70m² in total).
2) A MOIST LINING for dissolving gases.
3) Very THIN WALLS.
4) A COPIOUS BLOOD SUPPLY.

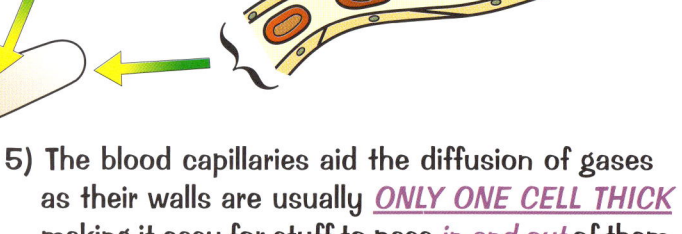

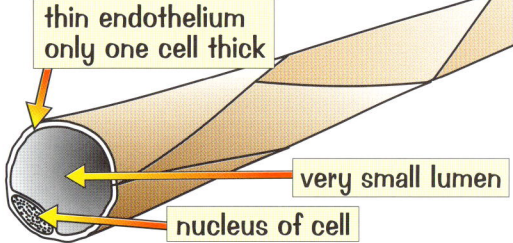

5) The blood capillaries aid the diffusion of gases as their walls are usually ONLY ONE CELL THICK making it easy for stuff to pass *in and out* of them.
6) To give you an idea of the size of things here — the capillaries are normally TOO SMALL to see.

This is a very Easy Page To Learn...

The big idea is that you should *understand and remember* what goes on and why it all works so well. A clear visual image in your head of these diagrams makes it a lot easier.
Learn the diagrams, words and all, until you can sketch them out *entirely from memory*.

NEAB SYLLABUS — SECTION ONE — LIFE PROCESSES & CELL ACTIVITY

Osmosis

Transport Across Boundaries

Osmosis is a Special Case of Diffusion, that's all

> OSMOSIS is the _movement of water molecules_ across a _partially permeable membrane_ from a region of HIGH WATER CONCENTRATION to a region of LOW WATER CONCENTRATION.

1) A _partially permeable membrane_ is just one with _real small holes_ in it. So small, in fact, that _only water_ molecules can pass through them, and bigger molecules like _glucose_ can't.
2) _Visking tubing_ is a partially permeable membrane that you should learn the _name_ of. It's also called _dialysis tubing_ because it's used in _kidney dialysis machines_.
3) The water molecules actually pass _both ways_ through the membrane in a _two-way traffic_.
4) But because there are _more on one side_ than the other there's a steady _net flow_ into the region with _fewer_ water molecules, i.e. into the _stronger solution_ (of glucose).
5) This causes the _glucose-rich_ region to fill up with _water_. The water acts like it's trying to _dilute_ it, so as to "_even up_" the concentration either side of the membrane.
6) OSMOSIS makes _plant_ cells _swell up_ if they're surrounded by _weak solution_ and they become TURGID. This is real useful for giving _support_ to green plant tissue and for _opening stomatal guard cells_.
7) _Animal_ cells don't have a _cell wall_ and can easily _burst_ if put into pure water because they _take in_ so much water _by osmosis_.

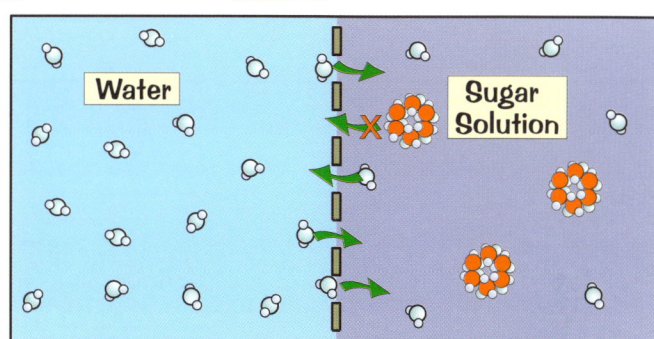

Net movement of water molecules

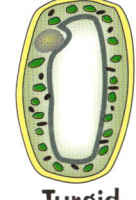
Turgid plant cell

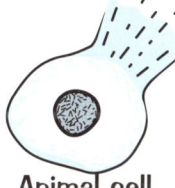
Animal cell bursting

Two Osmosis Experiments — Favourites for the Exams

① Potato Tubes

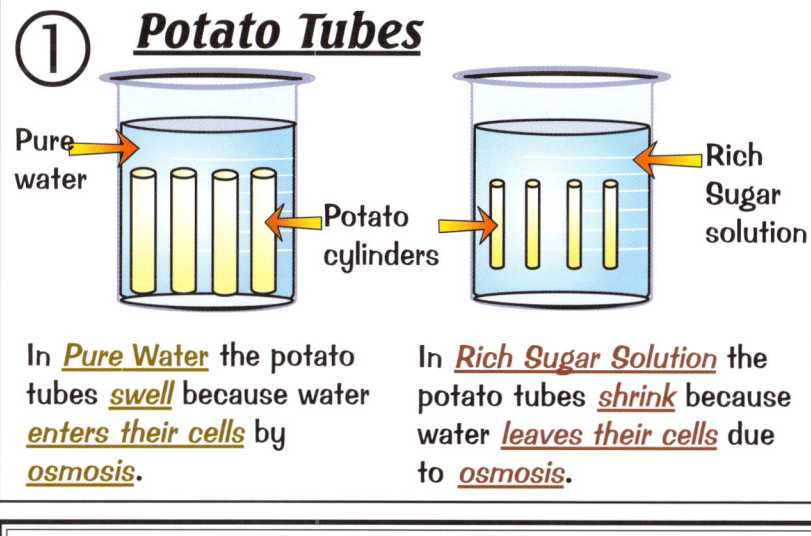

In _Pure_ Water the potato tubes _swell_ because water _enters their cells_ by _osmosis_.

In _Rich Sugar Solution_ the potato tubes _shrink_ because water _leaves their cells_ due to _osmosis_.

② Visking Tubing

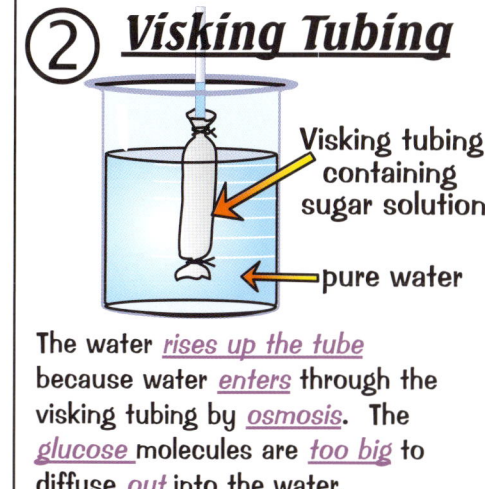

The water _rises up the tube_ because water _enters_ through the visking tubing by _osmosis_. The _glucose_ molecules are _too big_ to diffuse _out_ into the water.

Learn The facts about Osmosis...

Osmosis can be kind of confusing if you don't get to the bottom of it. In normal diffusion, glucose molecules move, but with small enough holes they can't. That's when only water moves through the membrane, and then it's called _osmosis_. Easy peasy, I'd say. _Learn and enjoy_.

Active Uptake

Transport Across Boundaries

Sometimes substances needed to be absorbed against the concentration gradient i.e. from a lower to a higher concentration. This process is lovingly referred to as ACTIVE UPTAKE.

Root Hairs take in Minerals using Active Uptake

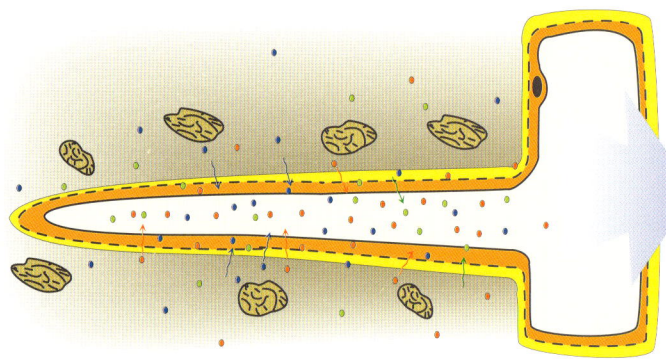

Root Hair cell

1) The cells on plant roots grow into long "hairs" which stick out into the soil.

2) This gives the plant a big surface area for absorbing water and minerals from the soil.

3) The concentration of minerals is higher in the root hair cell than in the soil around it.
4) So normal diffusion doesn't explain how minerals are taken up into the root hair cell.
5) They should go the other way if they followed the rules of diffusion.
6) The answer is that a conveniently mysterious process called "active uptake" is responsible.
7) Active uptake allows the plant to absorb minerals against the concentration gradient. This is essential for it's growth. But active uptake needs energy from respiration to make it work.
8) Active uptake also happens in humans, in taking glucose from the gut (see below), and from the kidney tubules (P. 31).

Small Food Molecules Can Diffuse into the Blood

These molecules (glucose, amino acids, fatty acids and glycerol) are small enough to diffuse into the blood.

In fact, these molecules will only "diffuse" into the blood with the help of active uptake (as used by plant root hairs) because the concentration gradient is the wrong way.

They then travel to where they're needed, and then diffuse out again. It's all clever stuff.

The small molecules diffuse into the blood...

..and then out again somewhere else...

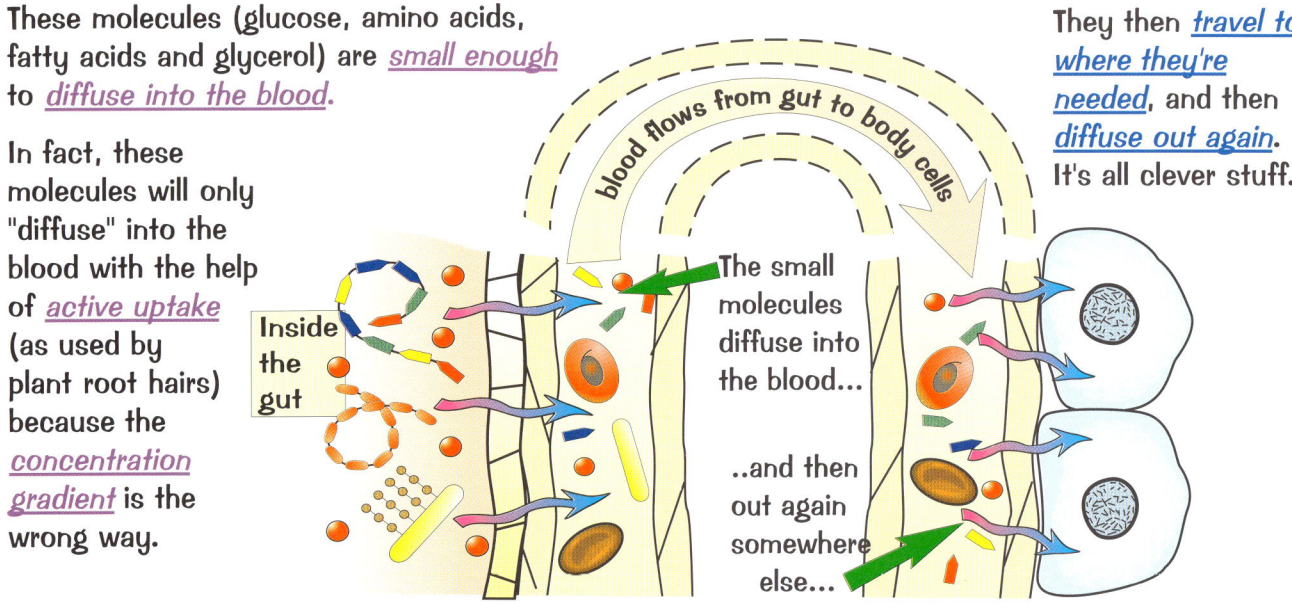

A Real Easy Page to Learn...

Make sure you can do these with the page covered up — if you can't, you ain't learnt nothin':
1) What type of molecules will diffuse through cell membranes and what type won't?
2) Give two examples of each.
3) Draw a full diagram of a root hair and say what it does.

NEAB Syllabus — SECTION ONE — LIFE PROCESSES & CELL ACTIVITY

Revision Summary For Section One

This is a short and easy section, that's for sure. But easy stuff means easy marks, and you better make sure you get all the easy marks — every last one. There's nothing quite as spectacularly dumb as working really hard at the difficult stuff and then forgetting about the easy bits. Here's some tough questions for you. Practise them over and over and over until you can just glide through them all, like a swan or something.

1) Name the seven things Mrs. Nerg helps you to remember. Give a brief definition of each one.
2) Copy the diagrams below and complete the labels adding a brief description for each one.

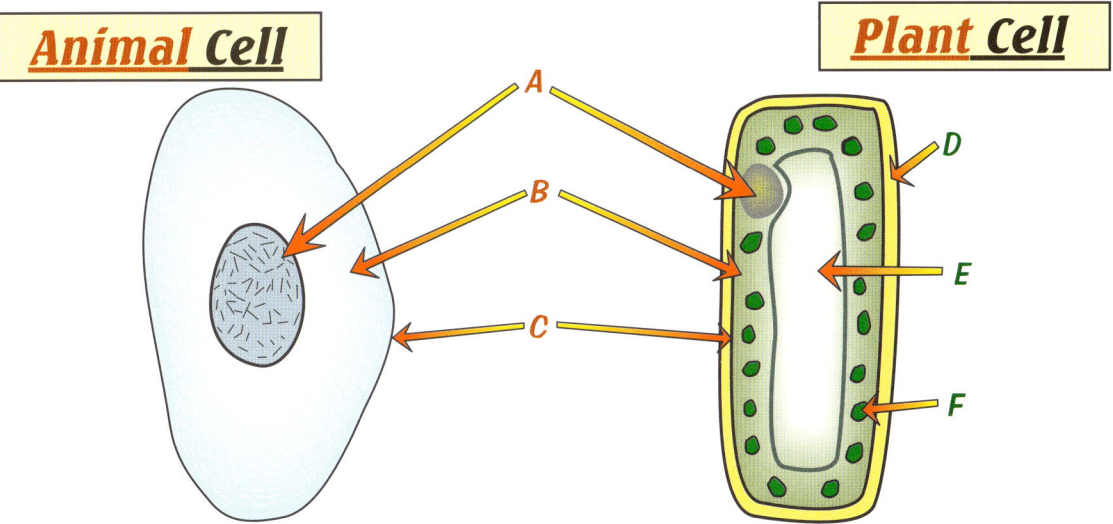

3) Sketch five specific plant cells.
4) Explain how each of the five cells is specialised.
5) Sketch five different animal cells and describe their specialised functions.
6) Give an example of this sequence: cells → tissues → organ → organism:
   a) in plants   b) in animals.
7) What specialisation is shared by all muscle tissue?
8) What role does glandular tissue play in the digestive system?
9) Sketch a xylem tube.
10) Label one feature of the xylem tube that helps plant support and one feature that helps water transport.
11) Sketch a villus and label its specialised features.
12) What two things give leaves such a large surface area?
13) What is this large surface area used for?
14) Give the strict definition of diffusion.
15) Sketch how a smell diffuses through air in a room.
16) Which three gases diffuse in and out of leaves? What process are they involved with?
17) Why are cell membranes kinda clever?
18) What will and won't diffuse through cell membranes?
19) Where in the body are the alveoli?
20) Name four specialisations that make alveoli an ideal exchange surface.
21) Give the full strict definition of osmosis.
22) What does osmosis do to plant and animal cells in pure water?
23) What is visking tubing? What will and won't pass through it?
24) Give full details of the potato tubes experiment and the visking tubing experiment.
25) What happens at root hairs? What process is involved? Which process *won't* work there?

SECTION ONE — LIFE PROCESSES & CELL ACTIVITY   NEAB SYLLABUS

Humans as Organisms

The Digestive System — Nutrition

You'll definitely get a question on this in your Exam so take your time and learn this very important diagram in all its infinite glory. And that includes the words too:

Ten Bits of Your Grisly Digestive System to Learn:

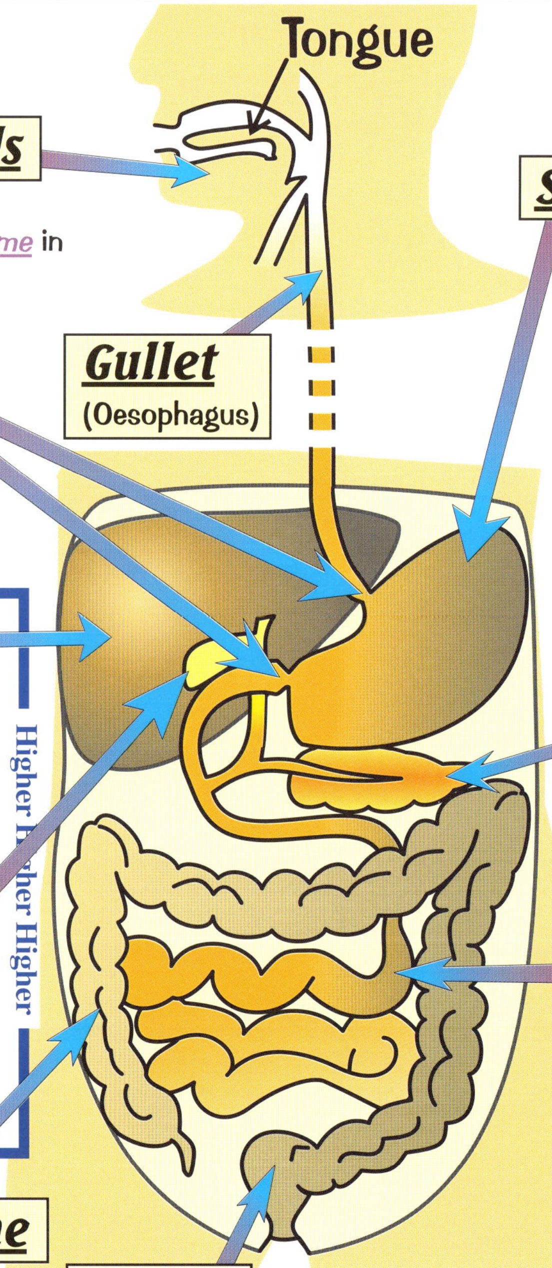

Tongue

Salivary Glands
These produce a CARBOHYDRASE enzyme in the SALIVA.

Stomach
1) It PUMMELS THE FOOD with its muscular walls.
2) It produces the PROTEASE enzyme.
3) It produces HYDROCHLORIC ACID for two reasons:
 a) To kill bacteria
 b) To give the right pH for the protease enzyme to work (pH2 - acidic).

Sphincters
Rings of muscle which are squeezed shut most of the time.

Gullet (Oesophagus)

Higher Higher Higher

Liver
Where BILE is produced. Bile EMULSIFIES FATS and neutralises stomach acid (to make conditions right for the enzymes in the small intestine).

Pancreas
Produces all three enzymes: PROTEASE, CARBOHYDRASE and LIPASE.

Gall bladder
Where bile is stored, before it's injected into the intestine.

Small intestine
1) Produces all the three enzymes: PROTEASE, CARBOHYDRASE and LIPASE.
2) This is also where the "food" is absorbed into the blood.
3) The inner surface is covered with villi to increase the surface area. It's also very long.

Large intestine
Where excess water is absorbed from the food.

Rectum
Where the faeces (made up mainly of indigestible food) are stored before they bid you a fond farewell through the anus.

Have You Learned The Whole Diagram?

The one thing they won't ask you to do in the Exam is draw the whole thing out yourself. BUT they will ask you about ANY part of it, e.g. "What is the position of the liver?", or "What does the pancreas produce?", or "What is the function of bile?" So in the end you have to learn the whole thing anyway. And that means being able to cover the page and draw it out, words and all. If you can't draw it all out from memory — then you haven't learnt it. Simple as that.

NEAB Syllabus — SECTION TWO — HUMANS AS ORGANISMS

Digestive Enzymes

Nutrition

There are only _THREE MAIN DIGESTIVE ENZYMES_. Sadly they all have silly names that can be hard to learn and their "products of digestion" all have suitably silly names too. Ah well — that's Biology for you!

Enzymes break down Big Molecules into Small Ones

1) _Starch_, _proteins_ and _fats_ are _big molecules_ which can't pass through cell walls into the blood.
2) _Sugars_, _amino acids_ and _fatty acids/glycerol_ are _much smaller molecules_ which can pass easily into the blood.
3) _Enzymes_ act as _catalysts_ to break down the _big molecules_ into the _smaller ones_.

1) Carbohydrase Converts Starch into Simple Sugars

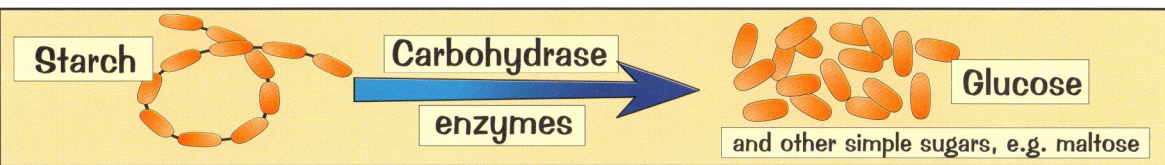

Carbohydrase is produced in _three_ places:
1) THE SALIVARY GLANDS (where it's called "amylase")
2) THE PANCREAS
3) THE SMALL INTESTINE

2) Protease Converts Proteins into Amino Acids

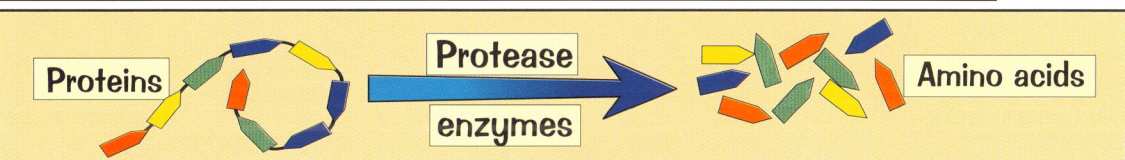

Protease is produced in _three_ places:
1) THE STOMACH (where it's called _pepsin_)
2) THE PANCREAS
3) THE SMALL INTESTINE

3) Lipase Converts Fats into Fatty Acids and Glycerol

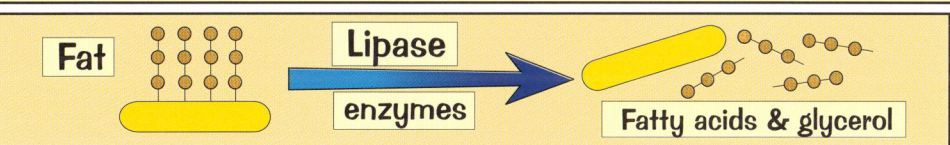

Lipase is produced in _two_ places:
1) THE PANCREAS
2) THE SMALL INTESTINE

BILE Neutralises The Stomach Acid and Emulsifies Fats

1) _IT'S ALKALINE_ to _neutralise the acid from the stomach_ to make conditions right for the enzymes in the small intestine to work.
2) _IT EMULSIFIES FATS_. In other words it breaks the fat into _tiny droplets_. This gives _a much bigger surface area_ of fat for the enzyme lipase to work on. Nothing too tricky there.

Yes, you have to know all that stuff too...

OK it's a pretty dreary page of boring facts, but it all counts — you're expected to know _every bit_ of information on this page. So, take a deep breath, _read it and learn it_, then _cover the page_ and _scribble it all down_. Then try again, and again... until you can do it. Fun isn't it.

SECTION TWO — HUMANS AS ORGANISMS

The Human Diet

Nutrition

There are <u>seven</u> different types of "<u>nutrients</u>" which all animals need in their diet. Make sure you know all about them:

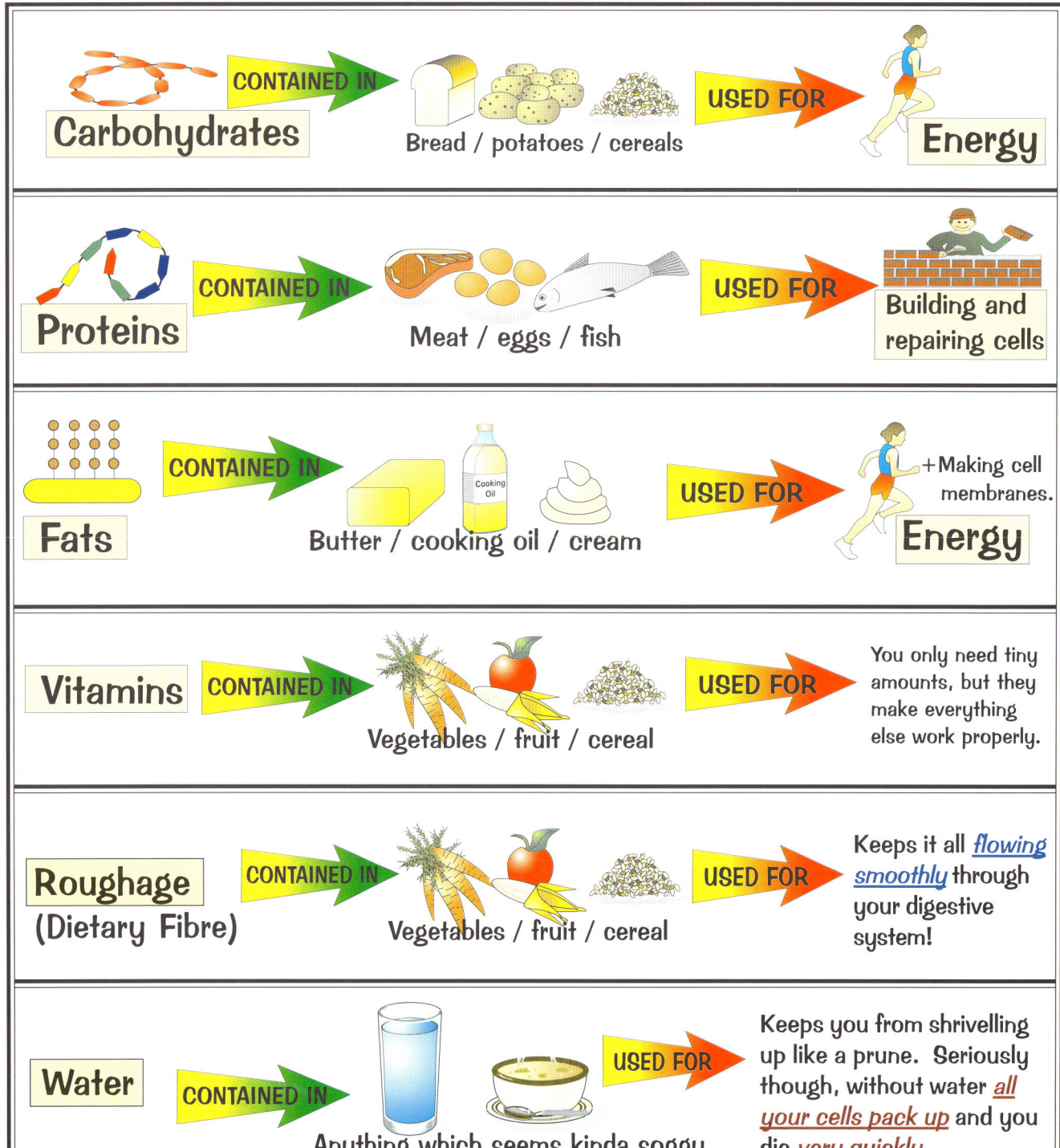

Well there's some food for thought anyway...

There's a fair bit of information on this page and any of it could come up in your Exam. <u>So sit and learn it</u>. Then turn the page and try and <u>scribble</u> it all down again. And just keep practising till you can answer these two questions without looking back.

1) What are the six different types of nutrient? What is each one used for in your body?
2) <u>For each one</u> name <u>three</u> foods which contain them.

NEAB Syllabus — SECTION TWO — HUMANS AS ORGANISMS

The Circulatory System

Circulation

The circulatory system's main function is to get food and oxygen to every cell in the body.
The diagram shows the basic layout, but make sure you learn the five important points too.

The DOUBLE Circulatory System, actually

① The HEART is actually TWO PUMPS.
The RIGHT SIDE pumps deoxygenated blood to the LUNGS to COLLECT OXYGEN.
Then the LEFT SIDE pumps this oxygenated blood AROUND THE BODY.

② ARTERIES carry blood *away from the heart* at HIGH PRESSURE.

③ Normally, arteries carry OXYGENATED BLOOD and veins carry DEOXYGENATED BLOOD.

④ The arteries eventually SPLIT OFF into *thousands of tiny capillaries* which take blood to *every cell in the body*.

⑤ The VEINS then collect the "used" blood and carry it *back to the heart* at *low pressure* to be pumped round again.

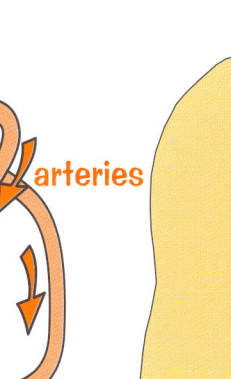

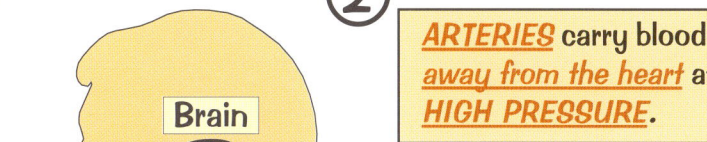

Fish don't have a double circulation system, but all fast-moving creatures like mammals and birds do. If you think about it, it's a mighty clever system to have evolved all by itself. Goodness knows how it ever happened.
I mean how could a single pump system "evolve" into a double one like this? It's got to be all or nothing for it to work hasn't it? That's quite a mutation, to go straight from a single pump heart that pumps to the lungs and then on to the rest of the body, to the double pump system shown above. But then life's full of little mysteries isn't it!

Let's See What You Know then...

At least this stuff on the circulatory system is fairly interesting. Mind you, there are still plenty of picky little details you need to be clear about. And yes, you've guessed it, there's one sure-fire way to check just how clear you are — *read it, learn it, then cover the page and reproduce it.*
Having to sketch the diagram out again *from memory* is the only way to *really learn it*.

SECTION TWO — HUMANS AS ORGANISMS   NEAB SYLLABUS

The Heart

Circulation

The heart is made almost entirely of _muscle_. And it's a _double pump_.
Visualise this diagram with its _bigger side_ full of _red, oxygenated blood_, and
its _smaller side_ full of _blue, deoxygenated blood_, and learn that the _left side_ is _bigger_.

Learn This Diagram of the Heart with All its Labels

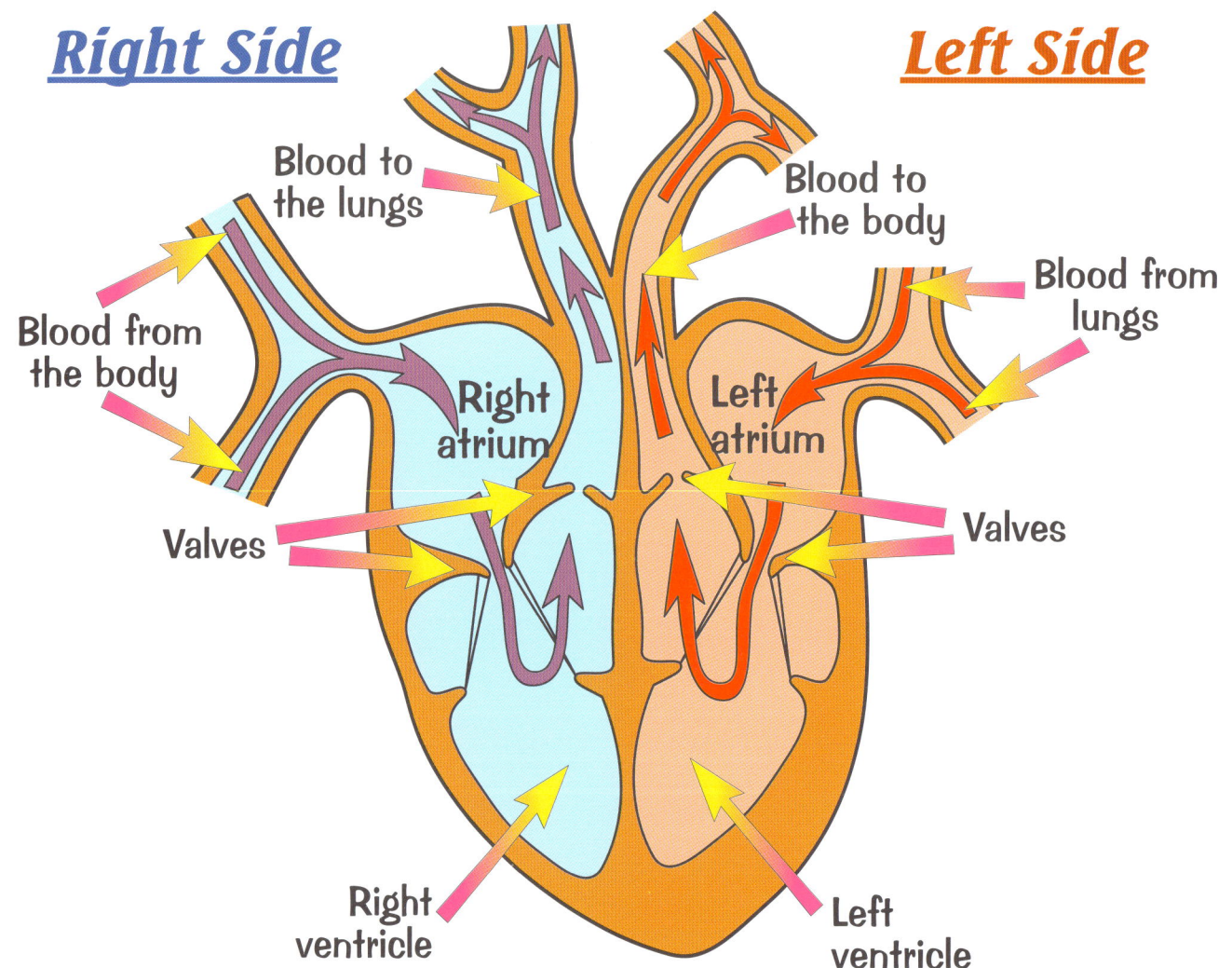

Four Extra Details to Delight and Thrill You

1) The _right side_ of the heart receives _deoxygenated blood_ from the body and pumps it only to the _lungs_, so it has _thinner walls_ than the left side.
2) The _left side_ receives _oxygenated blood_ from the lungs and pumps it out round the _whole body_, so it has _thicker, more muscular walls_.
3) The _ventricles_ are _much bigger_ than the _atria_ because they push blood _round the body_.
4) The _valves_ are for _preventing backflow_ of blood.

OK Let's get to the Heart of the Matter...

They quite often put a diagram of the heart in the Exam and ask you to label parts of it.
There's only one way to be sure you can label it all and that's to learn the diagram until you can
sketch it out, with all the labels, _from memory_. Also _learn_ the four points at the bottom.

The Pumping Cycle

Circulation

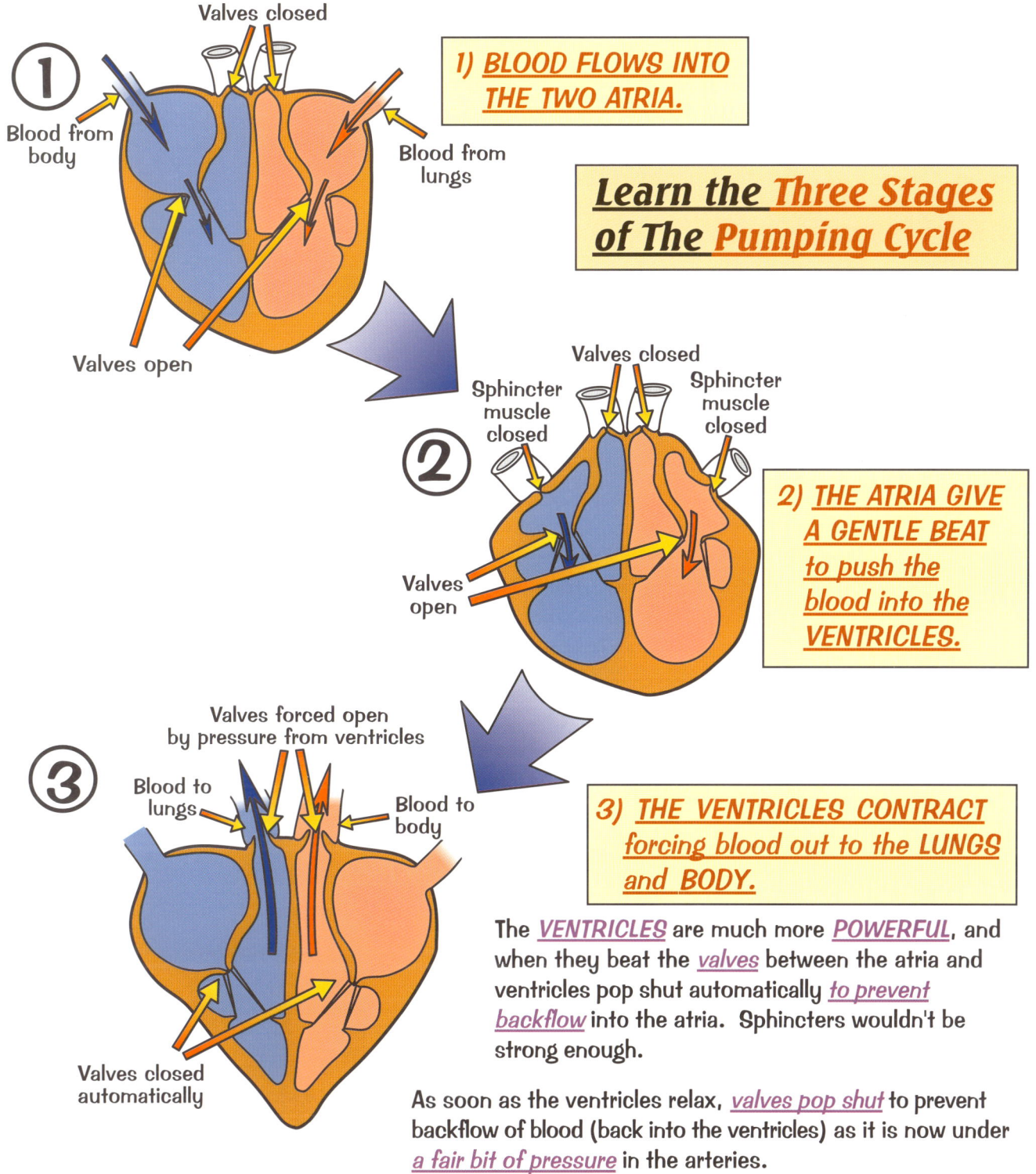

1) BLOOD FLOWS INTO THE TWO ATRIA.

Learn the **Three Stages** of The **Pumping Cycle**

2) THE ATRIA GIVE A GENTLE BEAT to push the blood into the VENTRICLES.

3) THE VENTRICLES CONTRACT forcing blood out to the LUNGS and BODY.

The VENTRICLES are much more POWERFUL, and when they beat the valves between the atria and ventricles pop shut automatically to prevent backflow into the atria. Sphincters wouldn't be strong enough.

As soon as the ventricles relax, valves pop shut to prevent backflow of blood (back into the ventricles) as it is now under a fair bit of pressure in the arteries.

4) THE BLOOD FLOWS DOWN THE ARTERIES, THE ATRIA FILL AGAIN AND THE WHOLE CYCLE STARTS OVER.

If this doesn't get your pulse racing, nothing will...

You need to know the details of each step of the pumping cycle. They will quite cheerfully give you a diagram similar to one of the above and ask you which valves are open or where the blood is flowing etc. etc. Make sure you can _sketch out_ all three diagrams _from memory_.

SECTION TWO — HUMANS AS ORGANISMS

Blood Vessels

Circulation

There are three different types of blood vessel and you need to know all about them:

Arteries Carry Blood Under Pressure

1) <u>ARTERIES</u> carry oxygenated blood <u>away from the heart</u>.
2) It comes out of the heart at <u>HIGH PRESSURE</u>, so the artery walls have to be <u>STRONG AND ELASTIC</u>.
3) Note how <u>THICK</u> the walls are compared to the size of the hole down the middle (the "lumen" — silly name!).

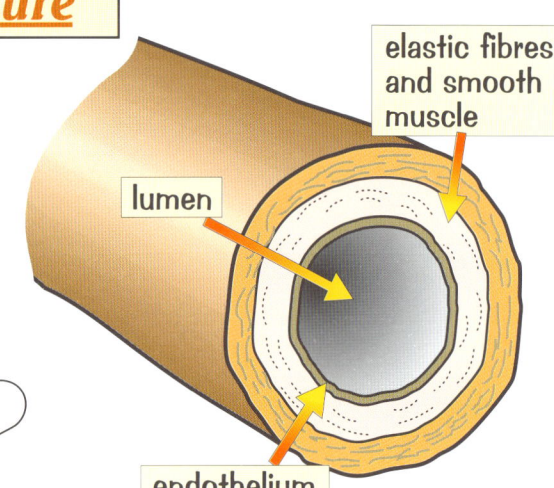

Capillaries are Real Small

1) Capillaries <u>deliver food and oxygen</u> direct to the body tissues and <u>take waste products away</u>.
2) Their walls are usually <u>ONLY ONE CELL THICK</u> to make it easy for stuff <u>to pass in and out of them</u>.
3) They are <u>TOO SMALL</u> to see.

Veins Take Blood Back to The Heart

1) <u>VEINS</u> carry <u>DEOXYGENATED BLOOD</u> back to the heart.
2) The blood is at <u>LOWER PRESSURE</u> in the veins so <u>the walls do not need to be so thick</u>.
3) They have a <u>BIGGER LUMEN</u> than arteries <u>TO HELP BLOOD FLOW</u>.
4) They also have <u>VALVES</u> to help keep the blood flowing <u>IN THE RIGHT DIRECTION</u>.

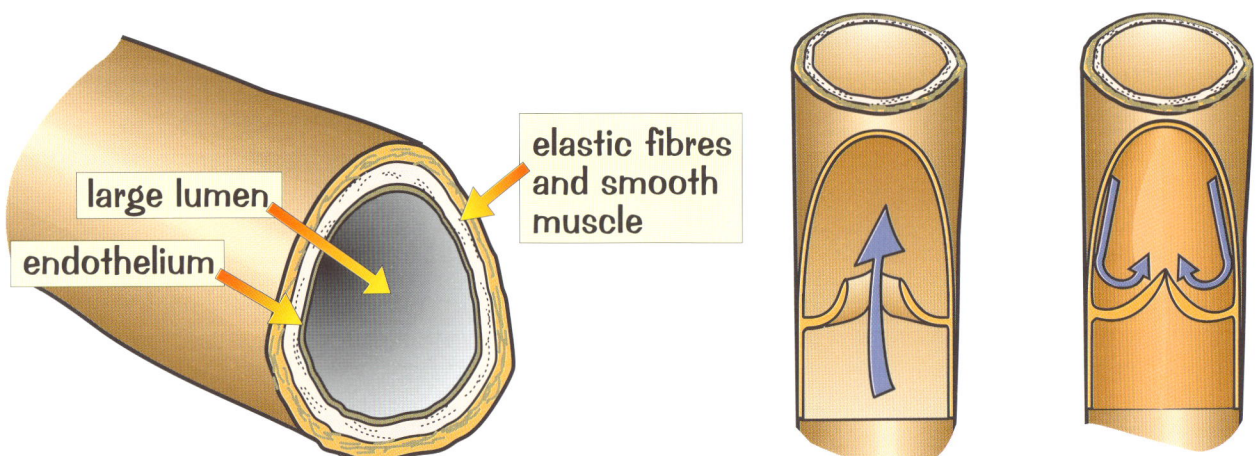

Don't Struggle in Vain...

Let's face it these are mighty easy diagrams to learn. Just make sure you learn the numbered points as well. I reckon it can't take more than two or three attempts before you can scribble out the whole of this page, diagrams and all, <u>entirely from memory</u>. <u>Concentrate on learning the bits you forgot each time</u>, of course. Try it and see how right I am!

Blood

Circulation

Plasma

This is a pale straw-coloured liquid which CARRIES JUST ABOUT EVERYTHING:
1) RED and WHITE BLOOD CELLS and PLATELETS.
2) Digested food products like GLUCOSE and AMINO ACIDS.
3) CARBON DIOXIDE from the organs to the lungs.
4) UREA from the liver to the kidneys.
5) HORMONES.
6) ANTIBODIES and ANTITOXINS produced by the white blood cells.

Red Blood Cells

1) Their job is to CARRY OXYGEN from the lungs to all the cells in the body.
2) They have a FLYING DOUGHNUT SHAPE to give MAXIMUM SURFACE AREA for absorbing oxygen.
3) They contain HAEMOGLOBIN which is very RED, and which contains a lot of IRON.
4) In the lungs, haemoglobin absorbs oxygen to become OXYHAEMOGLOBIN. In body tissues the reverse happens to release oxygen to the cells.
5) Red blood cells have NO NUCLEUS to make more room for haemoglobin.

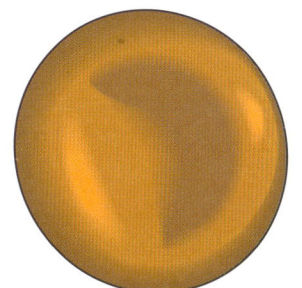
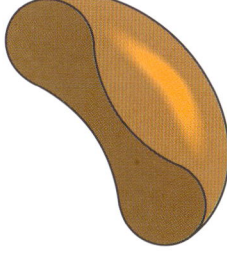

White Blood Cells

1) Their main role is DEFENCE AGAINST DISEASE.
2) They have a BIG NUCLEUS.
3) They GOBBLE UP UNWELCOME MICROBES.
4) They produce ANTIBODIES to fight bacteria.
5) They produce ANTITOXINS to neutralise the toxins produced by bacteria.

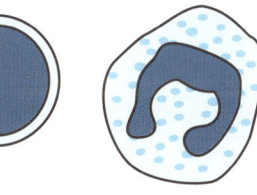

Platelets

1) These are SMALL FRAGMENTS OF CELLS.
2) They have NO NUCLEUS.
3) They HELP THE BLOOD TO CLOT at a wound.
 (So basically they just float about waiting for accidents to happen!)

More Blood, Sweat and Tears...

Do the same as usual — learn the facts until you can write them down from memory.

Just in case you think all this formal learning is a waste of time, how do you think you'd get on with these typical Exam questions if you didn't learn it all first?

THREE TYPICAL EXAM QUESTIONS:
1) What is the function of blood plasma? (4 marks)
2) What do white blood cells do? (3 marks)
3) What is the function of haemoglobin? (4 marks)

SECTION TWO — HUMANS AS ORGANISMS NEAB SYLLABUS

Lungs and Breathing

Breathing

The Thorax

Learn this diagram real good.

1) The THORAX is the top part of your 'body' which is protected by the RIBCAGE.

2) The LUNGS are like BIG PINK SPONGES.

3) The TRACHEA splits into two tubes called "BRONCHI" (each one is "a bronchus"), one going to each lung.

4) The bronchi split into progressively smaller tubes called BRONCHIOLES.

5) The bronchioles finally end at small bags called ALVEOLI where the gas exchange takes place.

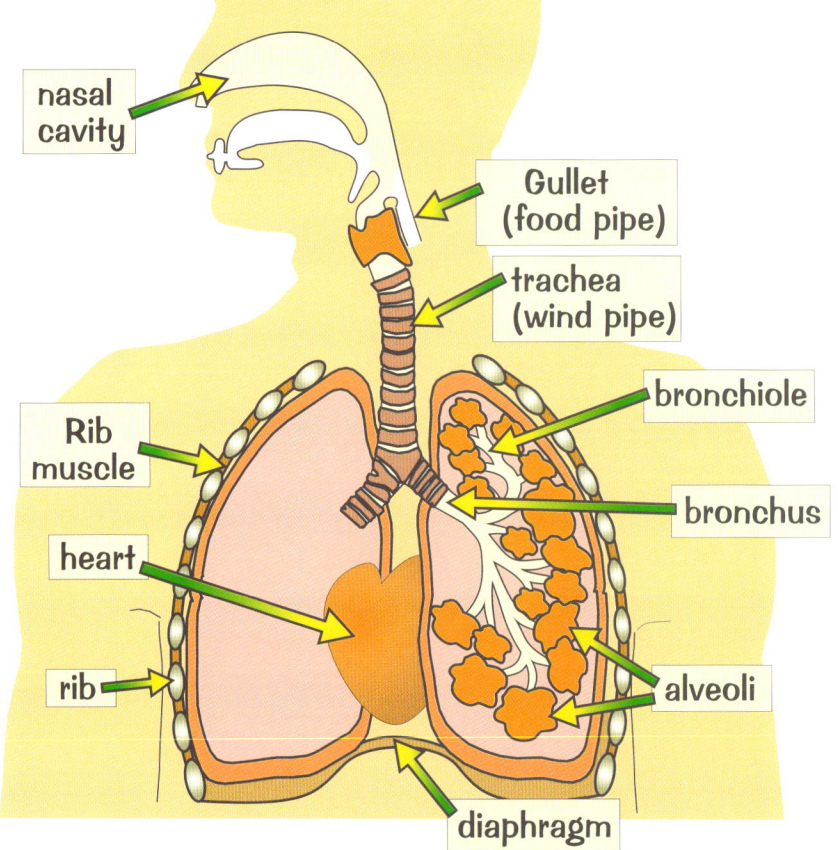

Breathing In...

1) *Rib muscles* and *diaphragm* CONTRACT.
2) *Thorax volume* INCREASES.
3) Air is DRAWN IN due to decreased pressure.

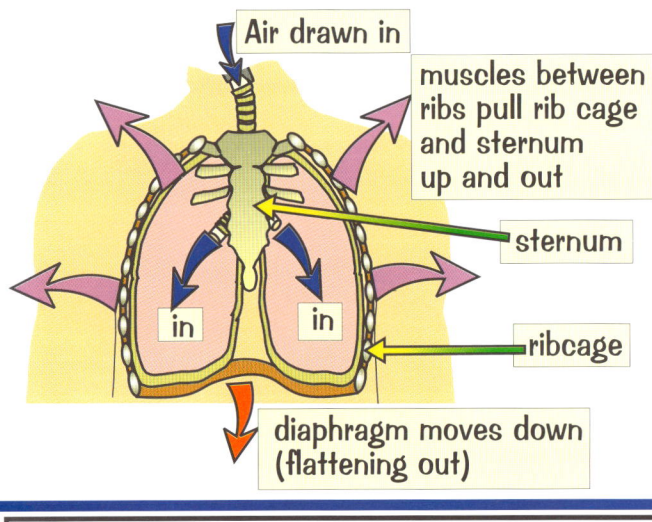

...and Breathing Out

1) *Rib muscles* and *diaphragm* RELAX.
2) *Thorax volume* DECREASES.
3) Air is FORCED OUT due to increased pressure.

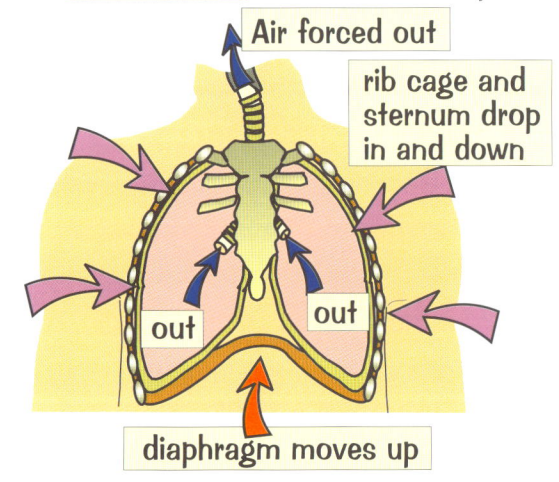

Higher Higher Higher

Stop Huffing and Puffing and just LEARN IT...

No dreary lists of facts this time anyway, just three splendid diagrams to learn.
When you practise repeating diagrams from memory, you don't have to draw them really neatly, just sketch them clear enough to label all the important bits. They would never ask you to draw a really fancy diagram in the Exam, but they will expect you to label one. But the only way to be sure you really know a diagram is to sketch it and label it, *all from memory*.

NEAB Syllabus   SECTION TWO — Humans as Organisms

Alveoli, Cells and Diffusion

Breathing

Alveoli

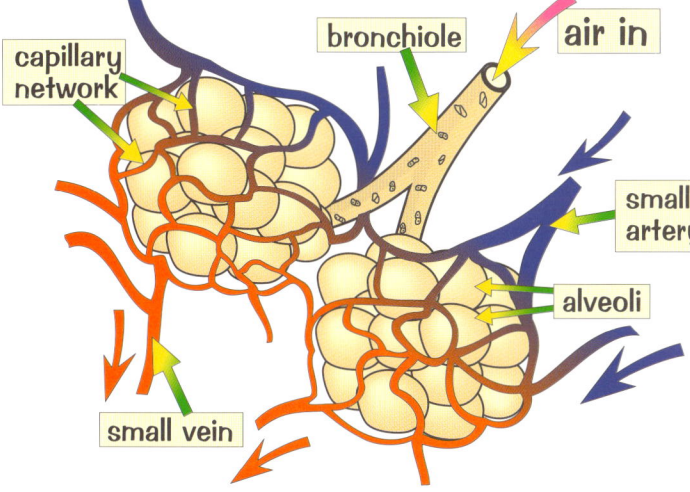

The ALVEOLI are an ideal EXCHANGE SURFACE. They have:

1) An ENORMOUS SURFACE AREA (about 70m² in total).
2) A MOIST LINING for dissolving gases.
3) Very THIN WALLS.
4) A COPIOUS BLOOD SUPPLY.

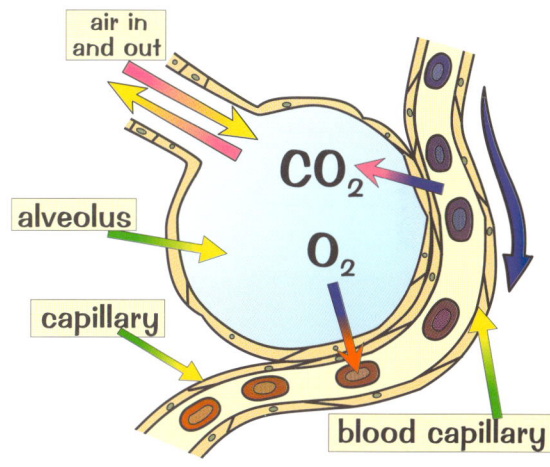

1) The job of the lungs is to *transfer OXYGEN to the blood* and to *remove waste CARBON DIOXIDE* from it.

2) To do this *the lungs contain millions of ALVEOLI* where *GAS EXCHANGE* takes place.

Gas Exchange at the Cells

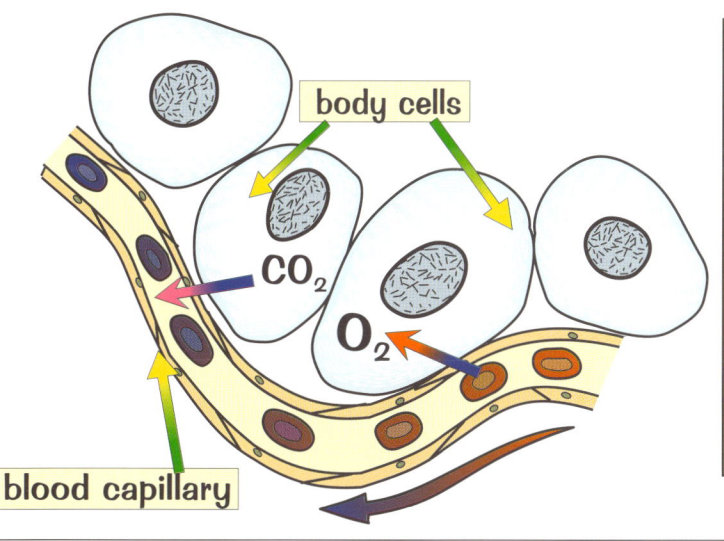

1) When the blood reaches the CELLS, OXYGEN IS RELEASED from the OXYHAEMOGLOBIN in the red blood cells AND DIFFUSES INTO THE BODY CELLS.

2) At the same time, CARBON DIOXIDE DIFFUSES INTO THE BLOOD (plasma) to be carried back to the lungs.

This is a very Easy Page To Learn...

Notice that the numbered points repeat information that the diagrams already show very clearly. The big idea is that you should *understand and remember* what goes on and why it all works so well. A clear visual image in your head of these diagrams makes it a lot easier.
Learn the diagrams, words and all, until you can sketch them out *entirely from memory*.

SECTION TWO — HUMANS AS ORGANISMS   NEAB SYLLABUS

Respiration

Respiration is NOT "breathing in and out"

1) Respiration is NOT breathing in and breathing out, as you might think.
2) Respiration actually goes on in every cell in your body.
3) Respiration is the process of converting glucose to energy.
4) It takes place in plants too. All living things "respire". They convert "food" into energy.

RESPIRATION is the process of CONVERTING GLUCOSE TO ENERGY, which goes on IN EVERY CELL

5) Energy released by respiration is used for four things:
   a) Build larger molecules from smaller ones
   b) enable muscle contraction
   c) maintain a steady body temperature
   d) power active transport

Aerobic Respiration Needs Plenty of Oxygen

1) Aerobic respiration is what happens if there's plenty of oxygen available.
2) "Aerobic" just means "with air" and it's the ideal way to convert glucose into energy.

You need to learn THE WORD EQUATION:

Glucose + Oxygen → Carbon Dioxide + Water + Energy

Anaerobic Respiration doesn't use Oxygen at all

1) Anaerobic respiration is what happens if there's no oxygen available.
2) "Anaerobic" just means "without air" and it's NOT the best way to convert glucose into energy.

You need to learn THE WORD EQUATION:

Glucose → Energy + Lactic Acid

3) Anaerobic respiration does not produce nearly as much energy as aerobic respiration — but it's useful in emergencies.

Fitness and the Oxygen Debt

1) When you do vigorous exercise and your body can't supply enough oxygen to your muscles they start doing anaerobic respiration instead.
2) This isn't great because the incomplete breakdown of glucose produces a build up of lactic acid in the muscles, which gets painful.
3) The advantage is that at least you can keep on using your muscles for a while longer.
4) After resorting to anaerobic respiration, when you stop you'll have an oxygen debt.
5) In other words you have to "repay" the oxygen which you didn't manage to get to your muscles in time, because your lungs, heart and blood couldn't keep up with the demand earlier on.
6) This means you have to keep breathing hard for a while after you stop to get oxygen into your muscles to convert the painful lactic acid to harmless CO_2 and water.

One Big Deep Breath and LEARN IT...

There are three sections on this page. Learning them well enough to scribble them down from memory isn't so difficult. You don't have to write it out word for word, just make sure you remember the important points about each bit.

The Eye

Nervous System

Learn The Eye with all its labels:

1) The tough outer _sclera_ has a transparent region at the front called the _cornea_.
2) The _pupil_ is the _hole_ in the middle of the _iris_, which the _light goes through_.
3) The size of the pupil is controlled by the _muscular_ iris.
4) The lens is held in position by _suspensory ligaments_ and _ciliary muscles_.
5) The _retina_ is the _light sensitive_ part and is covered in _receptor cells_.
6) Receptor cells send impulses to the brain along neurons in the _optic nerve_.

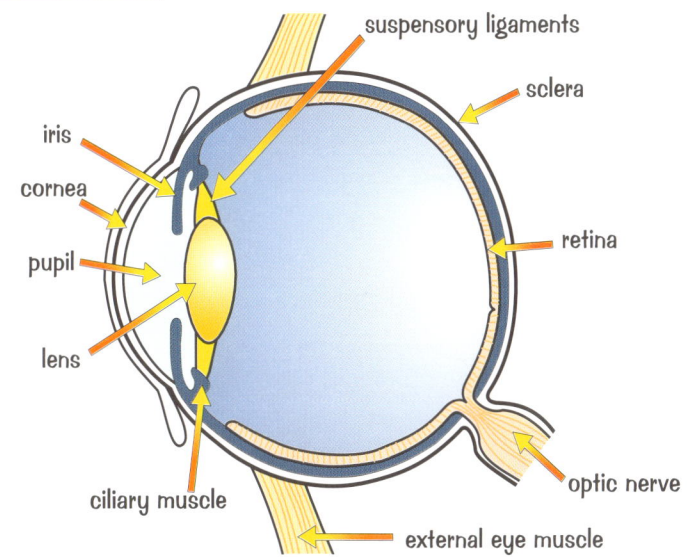

Focusing on Near and Distant Objects

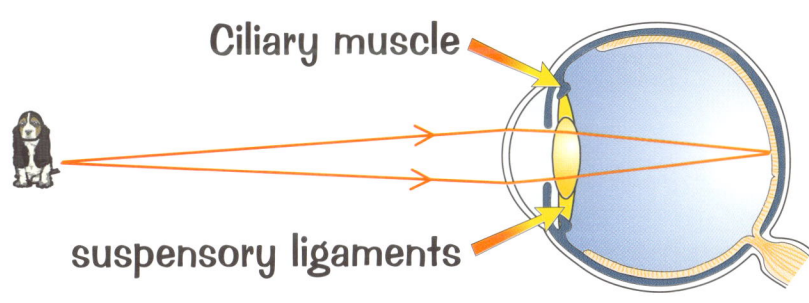

TO LOOK AT DISTANT OBJECTS:
1) The _ciliary muscles_ RELAX, which allows the _suspensory ligaments_ to PULL TIGHT.
2) This makes the lens go THIN.

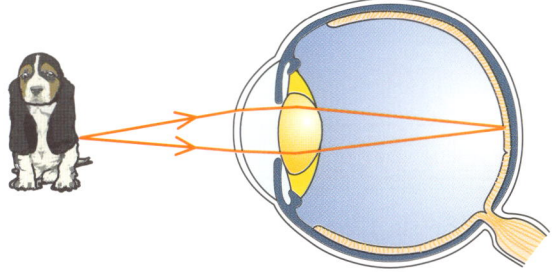

TO LOOK AT NEAR OBJECTS:
1) The _ciliary muscles_ CONTRACT which SLACKENS the _suspensory ligaments_.
2) The lens becomes FAT.

Let's See What You've Learned Then...

This is a pretty straightforward page of information. You need to make sure you know all the diagrams with all labels and also the numbered points for each.
Practise until you can _scribble_ the whole lot down _from memory_.

SECTION TWO — HUMANS AS ORGANISMS   NEAB Syllabus

The Nervous System

Nervous System

Sense Organs and Receptors

THE FIVE SENSE ORGANS ARE:
Eyes ears nose tongue skin

These five different <u>sense organs</u> all contain different <u>receptors</u>.

<u>Receptors</u> are groups of cells which are <u>sensitive to a stimulus</u> such as light or heat, etc.

SENSE ORGANS and RECEPTORS
Don't get them mixed up:

The <u>EYE</u> is a <u>SENSE ORGAN</u> — it contains <u>LIGHT RECEPTORS</u>.
The <u>EAR</u> is a <u>SENSE ORGAN</u> — it contains <u>SOUND-RECEPTORS</u>.

<u>RECEPTORS</u> are cells which <u>TRANSDUCE</u> energy (e.g. light energy) into <u>ELECTRICAL IMPULSES</u>.

The <u>FIVE SENSE ORGANS</u> and the <u>stimuli</u> that each one is <u>sensitive to</u>:

1) EYES
<u>Light</u> receptors.

2) EARS
<u>Sound</u> and "<u>balance</u>" receptors.

3) NOSE
<u>Taste</u> and <u>smell</u> receptors (Chemical stimuli).

4) TONGUE
<u>Taste</u> receptors:
Bitter, salt, sweet and sour (Chemical stimuli).

5) SKIN
<u>Touch</u>, <u>pressure</u>.

SENSORY NEURON
The <u>nerve fibres</u> that carry signals as <u>electrical impulses</u> from the <u>receptors</u> in the sense organs to the <u>central nervous system</u>.

THE CENTRAL NERVOUS SYSTEM
Consists of the <u>brain</u> and <u>spinal cord</u> only.

MOTOR NEURON
The <u>nerve fibres</u> that carry signals to the <u>effector</u> muscle or gland.

EFFECTORS
All your <u>muscles</u> and <u>glands</u> will respond to nervous impulses...

The Central Nervous System and Effectors

1) <u>THE CENTRAL NERVOUS SYSTEM</u> is where all the sensory information is sent and where reflexes and actions are coordinated. It consists of <u>THE BRAIN</u> and <u>SPINAL CORD</u> only.
2) <u>NEURONS</u> (nerve cells) <u>transmit electrical impulses</u> very quickly around the body.
3) The <u>EFFECTORS</u> are <u>muscles and glands</u> which respond to the various stimuli according to the instructions sent from the central nervous system.

This stuff is easy — I mean it's all just common senses...

There's quite a few names to learn here (as ever!).
But there's no drivel. It's all worth marks in the Exam, so learn it all.
Practise until you can <u>cover the page</u> and <u>scribble down</u> all the details <u>from memory</u>.

NEAB Syllabus   SECTION TWO — HUMANS AS ORGANISMS

Neurons and Reflexes

Nervous System

The Three Types of Neuron are All Much The Same

The THREE TYPES of NEURON are:
(They're all *pretty much the same*, they're just *connected to different things*, that's all.)

1) SENSORY neuron,
2) MOTOR neuron
3) RELAY neuron (or CONNECTOR neuron).

A Typical Neuron: — Learn the names of all the bits:

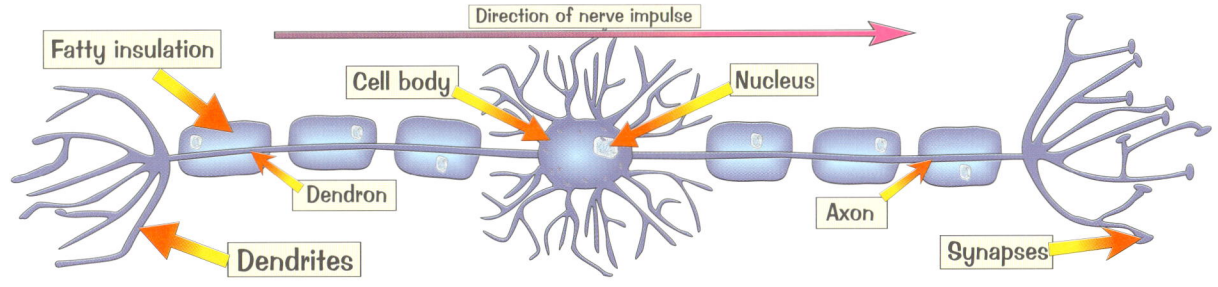

The Reflex Arc Allows Very Quick Responses

A Typical Reflex Arc

1. Cheeky bee stings finger
2. Stimulation of the pain receptor
3. Message travels along the sensory neuron
4. Message is passed along a relay neuron
5. Message travels along a motor neuron
6. When message reaches muscle, it contracts

A REFLEX ARC is simple enough. It's called an "arc" rather than a loop because the two ends don't connect.

1) The nervous system allows <u>very quick responses</u> because it uses <u>electrical impulses</u>.
2) <u>Reflex actions</u> are <u>automatic</u> (i.e. done without thinking) so they are <u>even quicker</u>.
3) Reflex actions save your body from <u>injury</u>, e.g. pulling your hand off a hot object for you.
4) A <u>muscle</u> responds by contracting, a <u>gland</u> responds by <u>secreting</u>.

Make sure you also learn the **BLOCK DIAGRAM** of a Reflex Arc:

Stimulus → Receptor → Sensory neuron → Relay neuron → Motor neuron → Effector → Response

Receptor cells

Synapses Use Chemicals

1) The <u>connection</u> between <u>two neurons</u> is called a <u>synapse</u>.
2) The nerve signal is transferred by <u>chemicals</u> which <u>diffuse</u> across the gap.
3) These chemicals then set off a <u>new electrical signal</u> in the <u>next</u> neuron.

A Synapse

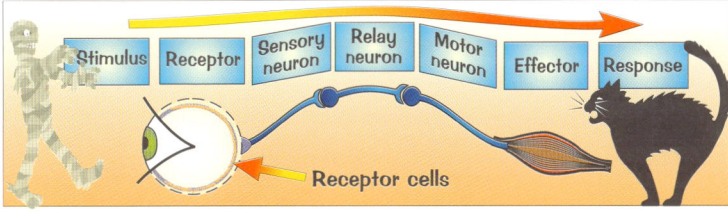

Don't get all twitchy — just learn it...

Another jolly page to learn, but it's all good clean fun. Once again, everything on this page is important information that you definitely need to know for the Exams. Use the diagrams to help you remember the important details. Then <u>cover the page</u> and <u>scribble it all down</u>.

SECTION TWO — HUMANS AS ORGANISMS   NEAB SYLLABUS

Hormones

Hormones are Chemical Messengers sent in the Blood

1) Hormones are CHEMICALS released DIRECTLY INTO THE BLOOD.
2) They are carried in the BLOOD PLASMA to other parts of the body.
3) They are produced in various GLANDS as shown on the diagram.
4) They TRAVEL ALL OVER THE BODY but only affect PARTICULAR CELLS in particular places.
5) The cells they affect are called TARGET CELLS.
6) They travel at "THE SPEED OF BLOOD".
7) They have LONG-LASTING EFFECTS.
8) They control things that need CONSTANT ADJUSTMENT.

LEARN THIS DEFINITION:

HORMONES ... are chemical messengers which travel in the blood to activate target cells.

THE PITUITARY GLAND
This produces many important hormones: LH, FSH and ADH.
These tend to control other glands, as a rule.

PANCREAS
Produces insulin and glucagon for the control of blood sugar.

OVARIES — females only
Produce oestrogen which promotes all female secondary sexual characteristics during puberty:
1) Extra hair in places.
2) Changes in body proportions.
3) Egg production.

ADRENAL GLAND
Produces adrenaline which prepares the body with the well known fight or flight reaction:
Increased blood sugar, heart rate, breathing rate, and diversion of blood from skin to muscles.

TESTES — males only
Produce testosterone which promotes all male secondary sexual characteristics at puberty:
1) Extra hair in places.
2) Changes in body proportions.
3) Sperm production.

Hormones and Nerves do Similar Jobs, but there are Important Differences

NERVES:
1) Very FAST message.
2) Act for a very SHORT TIME.
3) Act on a very PRECISE AREA.
4) IMMEDIATE reaction.

HORMONES:
1) SLOWER message.
2) Act for a LONG TIME.
3) Act in a more GENERAL way.
4) LONGER-TERM reaction.

Hormones — Easy peasy...

Well let's face it, there's not much to learn here is there? The diagram and all its labels are easy enough, and so's the comparison of nerves and hormones. The definition of hormones is worth learning word for word. The eight points at the top of the page are best done with the good old "mini-essay" method. Learn it, cover the page and scribble. Then try again. And smile of course.

Insulin and Diabetes

Hormones

Insulin and *glucagon* are *hormones* which control how much *sugar* there is in your *blood*. LEARN how:

Insulin and Glucagon Control Blood Sugar Levels

1) Eating *carbohydrate* foods puts a lot of *glucose* into the blood from the *gut*.
2) *Normal metabolism* of cells *removes glucose* from the blood.
3) Vigorous *exercise* removes *much more* glucose from the blood.
4) Obviously, to keep the *level* of blood glucose *controlled* there has to be a way to *add or remove* glucose from the blood. This is achieved by two hormones "*insulin*" and "*glucagon*" which are released by the *pancreas*.

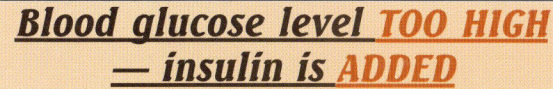

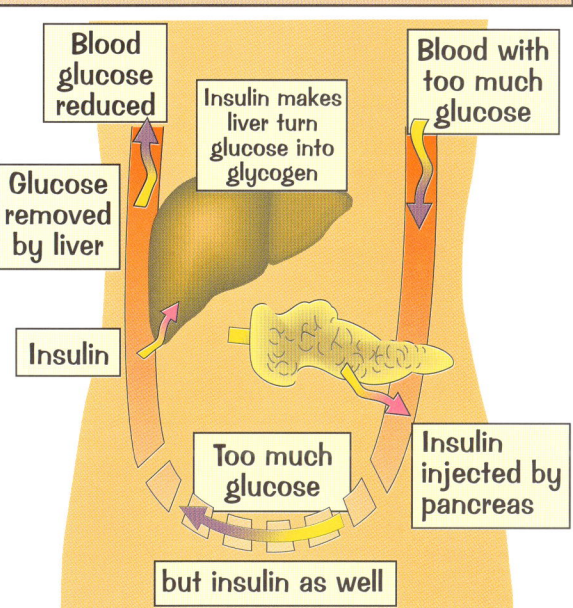

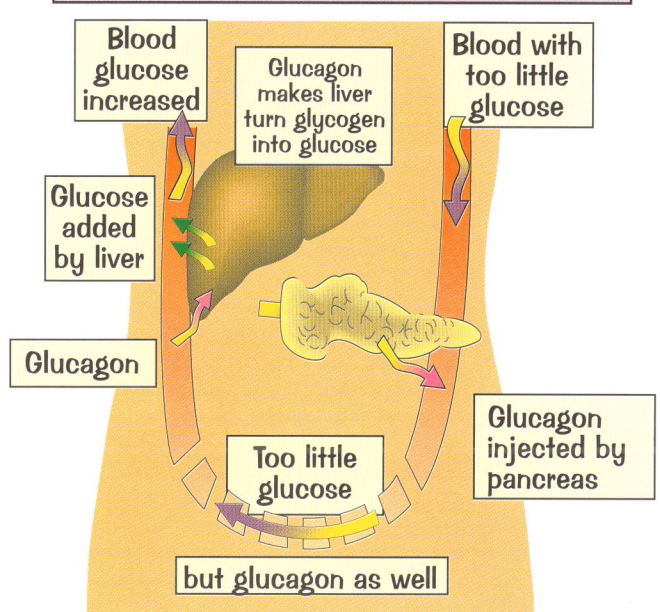

Remember, the addition of *insulin reduces* the blood sugar level and the addition of *glucagon increases* the blood sugar level.

Diabetes — the Pancreas Stops Making Enough Insulin

1) *Diabetes is a disease* in which *the pancreas doesn't produce enough insulin*.
2) The result is that a person's *blood sugar can rise to a level that can kill them*.
3) The problem can be *controlled* in *two ways*:

A) *Avoiding foods rich in carbohydrate* (which turns to glucose when digested). It can also be helpful to take *exercise* after eating carbohydrates... i.e. trying to *use up* the *extra glucose* by doing *physical activity*, but this isn't usually very practical.

B) *INJECTING INSULIN INTO THE BLOOD* before meals (especially if high in carbohydrates). This will make the liver *remove the glucose* from the blood *as soon as it enters it* from the gut, when the (carbohydrate-rich) food is being *digested*. This stops the level of glucose in the blood from getting too high and is a *very effective treatment*.

Learn all this stuff about blood sugar and diabetes...

This stuff on blood sugar and insulin can seem a bit confusing at first, but if you concentrate on learning those two diagrams, it'll all start to get a lot easier. Don't forget that only carbohydrate foods put the blood sugar levels up. *Learn it all*, then *cover the page* and *scribble it all down*.

SECTION TWO — HUMANS AS ORGANISMS NEAB SYLLABUS

Female Menstrual Cycle

Hormones

1) The _monthly_ release of an _egg_ from a woman's _ovaries_ and the build up and break down of a protective lining in the _womb_ is called the _menstrual cycle_.

2) _Hormones_ released by the _pituitary gland_ (P. 24) and the _ovaries_ control the different stages of the menstrual cycle.

The Menstrual Cycle has Four Stages

STAGE 1 _Day 1 is when the bleeding starts_. The uterus lining breaks down for about four days.

STAGE 2 _The lining of the womb builds up again_, from day 4 to day 14, into a thick spongy layer of blood vessels ready to receive a fertilised egg.

STAGE 3 _An egg is developed and then released_ from the ovary at day 14.

STAGE 4 _The wall is then maintained_ for about 14 days, until day 28. If no fertilised egg has landed on the uterus wall by day 28 then the spongy lining starts to break down again and the whole cycle starts over. The diagram below illustrates this.

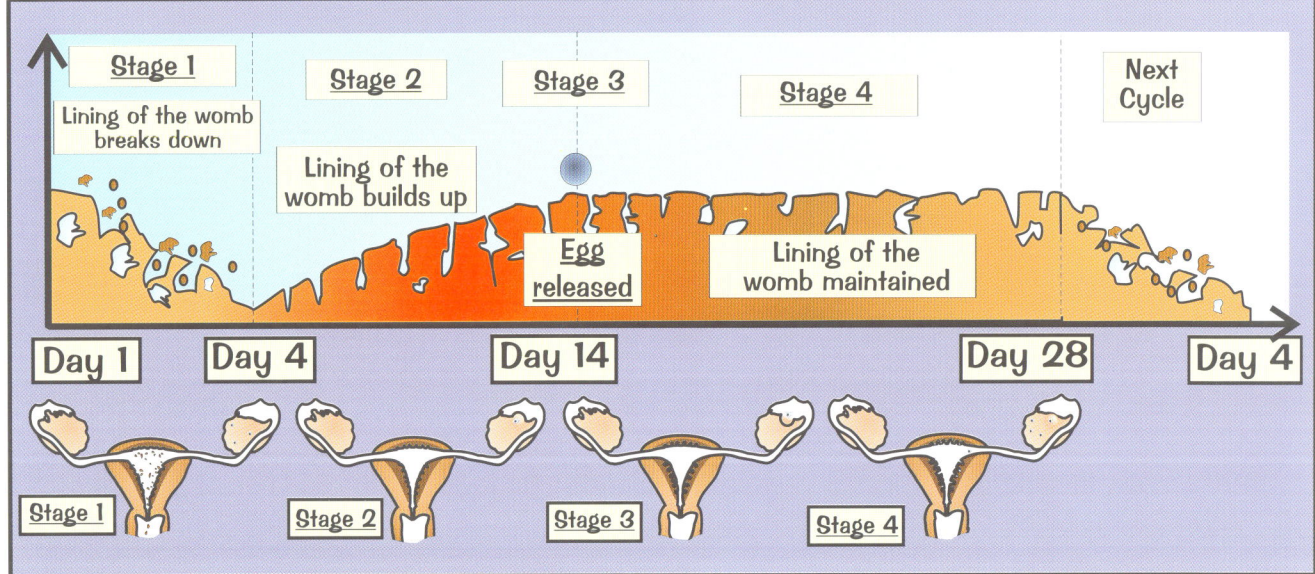

The control of Fertility

Women who want to control their fertility can be given controlled doses of hormones involved in the menstrual cycle.

1) **FERTILITY DRUGS** contain hormones that _stimulate_ the release of the egg from the ovaries. But you do have to be _careful_ with the _dosage_ of these drugs or too many eggs can be released resulting in _multiple births_.

2) **CONTRACEPTIVE DRUGS** contain hormones that _prevent_ the release of eggs from the ovaries. These drugs also have their _drawbacks_. They can produce _side-effects_ such as headaches and nausea and are _not_ 100% effective at preventing pregnancy.

Female or otherwise, you've still gotta learn it...

This is the relatively simple stuff on the menstrual cycle and it's definitely well worth learning. Make sure you know what the hormones do and where they are produced, and also how hormones are used to control fertility. _Learn and enjoy_.

Menstrual Cycle Hormones

Hormones

There are Three Main Hormones involved

1) FSH (Follicle Stimulating Hormone):

1) Produced by the pituitary gland.
2) Causes an egg to develop in one of the ovaries.
3) Stimulates the ovaries to produce oestrogen.

2) OESTROGEN:

1) Produced in the ovaries.
2) Causes pituitary to produce LH.
3) Inhibits the further release of FSH.

3) LH (Luteinising Hormone):

1) Produced by the pituitary gland.
2) Stimulates the release of an egg at around the middle of the menstrual cycle.

Oestrogen and FSH can both be used to artificially control fertility (see below).

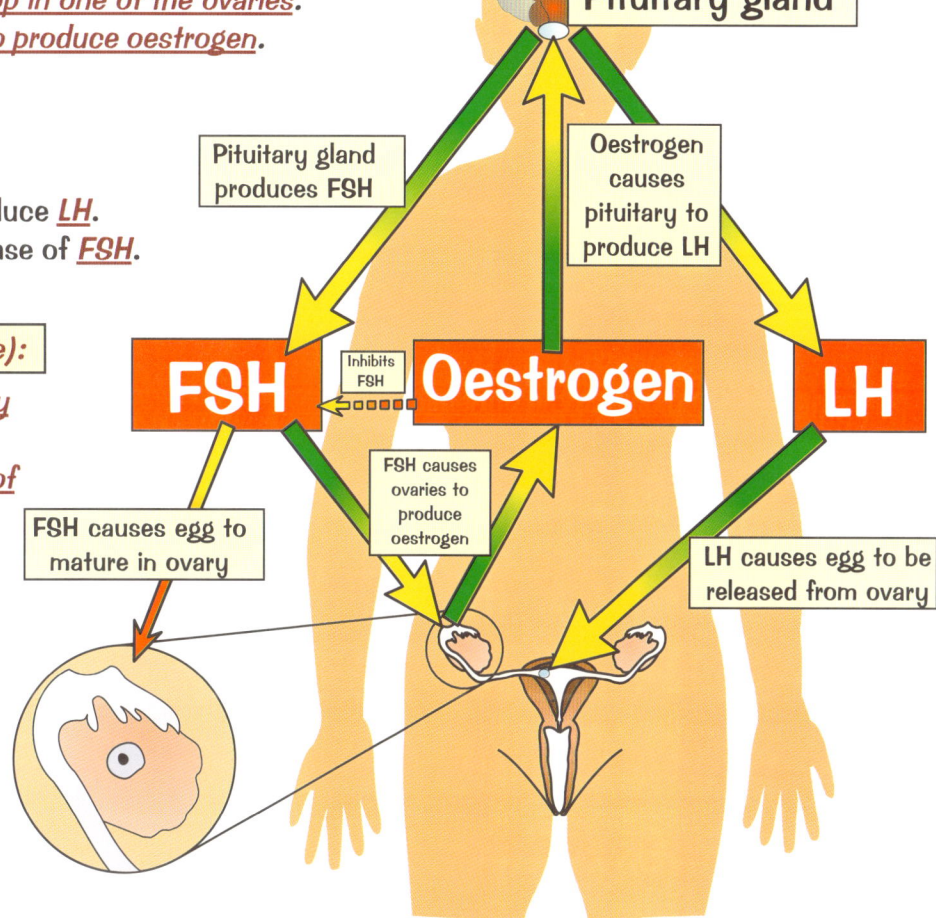

Oestrogen is Used to Stop Egg Production in "The PILL"

1) "THE PILL", as it's cheerfully known is an oral contraceptive that contains oestrogen.
2) It may seem kind of strange but even though oestrogen stimulates the release of eggs, if oestrogen is taken every day to keep the level of it permanently high, it inhibits the production of FSH and after a while egg production stops and stays stopped.

FSH is Used to Stimulate Egg Production in Fertility Treatment

1) A hormone called FSH can be taken by women (who have low levels of FSH) to stimulate egg production in their ovaries.
2) In fact FSH (Follicle Stimulating Hormone) stimulates the ovaries to produce oestrogen which in turn stimulates the release of an egg.

Well, you gotta be pretty keen to get your head round that lot!

I have to say it's pretty difficult to get a full understanding of how these three hormones all interact with each other to perpetuate the monthly cycle. Basically, as each hormone increases, it causes one event or another, and at the same time either promotes or inhibits the production of one of the other hormones. That's how it all keeps going in a cycle, but it's real tricky to understand. So just how keen are you?

SECTION TWO — HUMANS AS ORGANISMS

NEAB SYLLABUS

Homeostasis

Homeostasis

Homeostasis is a fancy word. It covers lot of things, so I guess it has to be. Homeostasis covers all the functions of your body which try to maintain a "constant internal environment". Learn the definition:

HOMEOSTASIS — the maintenance of a CONSTANT INTERNAL ENVIRONMENT

There are *six different bodily levels* that need to be controlled:

1) REMOVAL OF CO_2
2) REMOVAL OF UREA
⇐ These two are WASTES. They're constantly produced in the body and you just need to get rid of them.

3) ION content
4) WATER content
5) SUGAR content
6) TEMPERATURE
⇐ These four are all "GOODIES" and we need them, BUT AT JUST THE RIGHT LEVEL — not too much and not too little.

All your body's cells are BATHED IN TISSUE FLUID, which is just blood plasma which has leaked out of the capillaries (on purpose).

To keep all your cells working properly, *this fluid must be just right* — in other words, THE SIX THINGS above must be KEPT AT THE RIGHT LEVEL — not too high, and not too low.

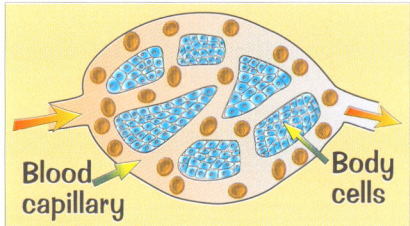
Blood capillary — Body cells

Learn the Organs Involved in Homeostasis:

THE BRAIN
1) Contains receptors to monitor blood temperature and water content and then sends nerve impulses to the skin and to the pituitary gland.
2) It also monitors CO_2 levels.

THE LUNGS
These remove CO_2 and some of the excess water.

THE KIDNEYS
Remove urea. They also adjust the ion and water content of the blood.

THE BLADDER
This is where urine is stored before departure.

PITUITARY GLAND
Produces many vital hormones, including ADH, for controlling water content.

THE SKIN
This removes water through sweat and adjusts the body temperature, with the help of...

THE MUSCLES
which can produce heat if necessary (by shivering).

THE LIVER
THE PANCREAS
These two work together to adjust blood sugar level.

Fingers not needed for homeostasis.

Learn about Homeostasis — and keep your cool...

This is all a bit technical. Homeostasis is really quite a complicated business. It's just a good job it does it automatically or we'd all be in real trouble. You still gotta *learn it* for your Exam though. *Scribble*.

Skin and Temperature

Homeostasis

Controlling Our Body Temperature

All _enzymes_ work best at a certain temperature. The enzymes within the human body work best at about _37°C_.

When you're too COLD your body SHIVERS (increasing your metabolism) to produce heat.

When you're too HOT you produce SWEAT which cools you down.

1) There is a _thermoregulatory centre_ in the _brain_ which acts as your own _personal thermostat_.
2) It contains receptors that are sensitive to the blood temperature in the brain.
3) The thermoregulatory (there's that long word again) centre also receives impulses from the skin.
4) These impulses provide information about _skin temperature_.

The Skin has Three Tricks for Altering Body Temperature

1) The ENZYMES in the cells of the human body work best at 37°C.
2) The THERMOREGULATORY CENTRE senses changes and sends NERVOUS IMPULSES to the skin.
3) THE SKIN then has _three tricks_ for _controlling body temperature_:

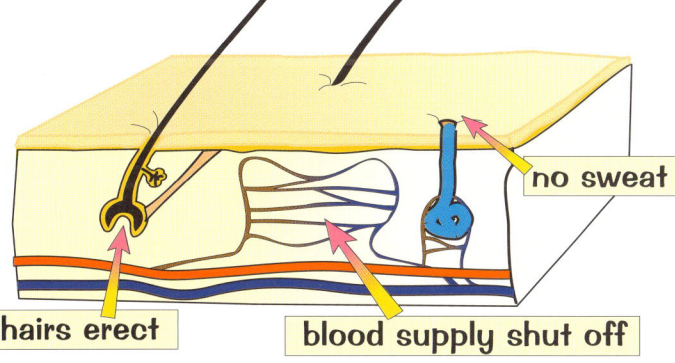

When you're TOO COLD:
1) HAIRS stand on end to keep you warm.
2) NO SWEAT is produced.
3) The BLOOD SUPPLY to the skin CLOSES OFF.

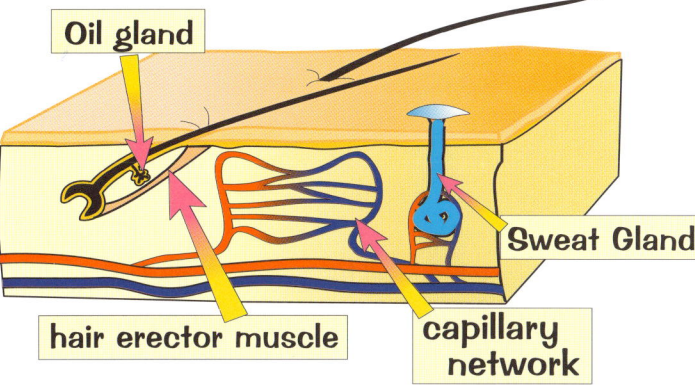

When you're TOO HOT:
1) HAIRS lie flat.
2) SWEAT is produced which evaporates to cool you down.
3) The BLOOD SUPPLY to the skin opens up to release body heat.

So much to learn — don't let it get under your skin...

I can count about 13 important facts to learn on this page, plus a couple of suitably splendid diagrams. _Learn the headings_ for each section, then _cover the page_ and _scribble_ out the details.

SECTION TWO — HUMANS AS ORGANISMS   NEAB SYLLABUS

Kidneys

Homeostasis

Kidneys basically act as filters to "clean the blood"

The _kidneys_ perform _three main roles_:

1) _Removal of urea_ from the blood.
2) _Adjustment of ions_ in the blood.
3) _Adjustment of water content_ of the blood.

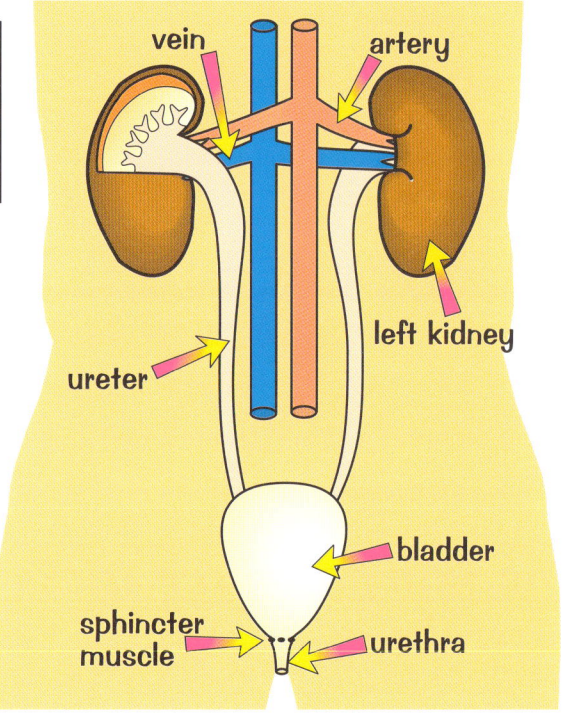

1) Removal of Urea

1) _Urea_ is produced in the _liver_.
2) Proteins can't be _stored_ by the body so _excess amino acids_ are _broken down_ by the liver into fats and carbohydrates.
3) The _waste product_ is _urea_ which is passed into the blood to be _filtered out_ by the _kidneys_. Urea is also lost partly in _sweat_. Urea is _poisonous_.

2) Adjustment of Ion Content

1) _Ions_, such as sodium are taken into the body in _food_, and then absorbed into the blood.
2) Excess ions are _removed_ by the kidneys. For example, a salty meal will contain far too much and the kidneys will _remove the excess_ from the blood.
3) Some ions are also lost in _sweat_ (which tastes salty, you'll have noticed).
4) But the important thing to remember is that the _balance_ is always maintained by the _kidneys_.

3) Adjustment of Water Content

Water is _taken in_ to the body as _food and drink_ and is _lost_ from the body in _three ways_:
   1) in URINE   2) in SWEAT   3) in BREATH

There's a need for the body to _constantly balance_ the water coming in against the water going out. The amount lost in the _breath_ is fairly _constant_, which means the _water balance_ is between:
   1) Liquids _consumed_
   2) Amount _sweated out_
   3) Amount _dumped by the kidneys_ in the _urine_.

ON A COLD DAY, if you _don't sweat_, you'll produce _more urine_ which will be _pale and dilute_.
ON A HOT DAY, you _sweat a lot_, your urine will be _dark-coloured_, _concentrated_ and _little of it_.
The water lost when it is hot has to be taken taken in as food and drink to restore the balance.

How Much Do You Know About Kidneys? — Let's See...

Do the usual thing — sit and _learn it_, then _cover the page_ and _sketch out the diagrams_ and _scribble down_ all the important details. Then try again, and again, until you get it all.
I hope it's obvious that you only scribble out very rough diagrams — just to show the details.

Ultrafiltration and ADH

Homeostasis

Three Stages of Filtration in the Kidneys

1) Ultrafiltration:

1) A _high pressure_ is built up which _squeezes water_, _urea_, _ions_ and _glucose_ out of the blood and into the _kidney tubule_.
2) However, _big molecules_ like _proteins_ are _not squeezed out_. They stay in the blood.

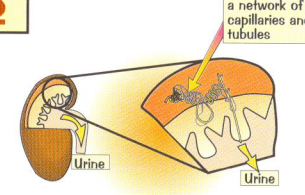

2) Reabsorption:

Useful substances are reabsorbed:
1) _All the sugar_ is reabsorbed. This involves the process of _active uptake_.
2) _Sufficient ions_ are reabsorbed. Excess ions are not. _Active uptake_ is needed.
3) _Sufficient water_ is reabsorbed, according to the level of the hormone _ADH_ (see below).

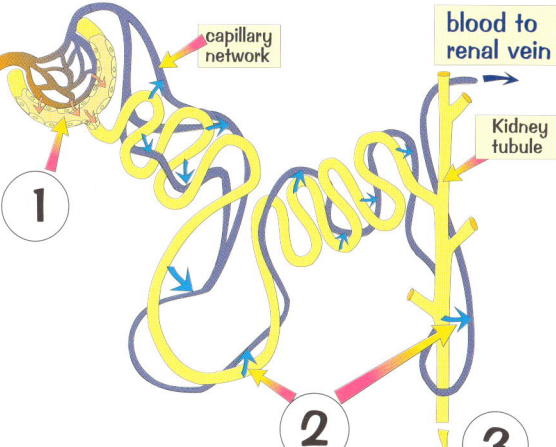

3) Release of wastes:

1) All _urea_ and _excess ions and water_ are _not reabsorbed_.
2) These continue _out of the kidney_, into the ureter and down to the _bladder_ as _urine_.

ADH (Anti Diuretic Hormone) — Water Regulation

The brain _monitors the water content of the blood_ and instructs the PITUITARY GLAND to release ADH into the blood _accordingly_, as shown below:

Too Little Water in Blood

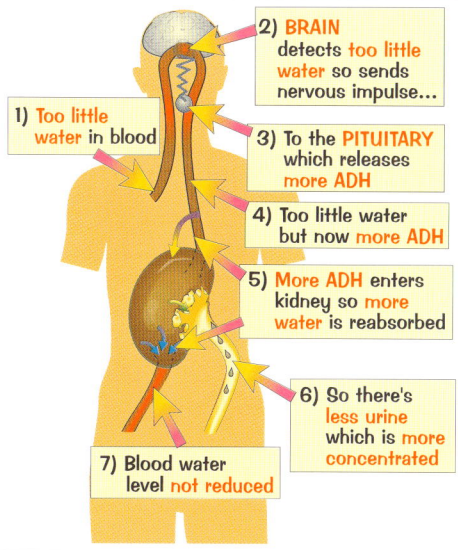

1) Too little water in blood
2) BRAIN detects too little water so sends nervous impulse...
3) To the PITUITARY which releases more ADH
4) Too little water but now more ADH
5) More ADH enters kidney so more water is reabsorbed
6) So there's less urine which is more concentrated
7) Blood water level not reduced

Too Much Water in Blood

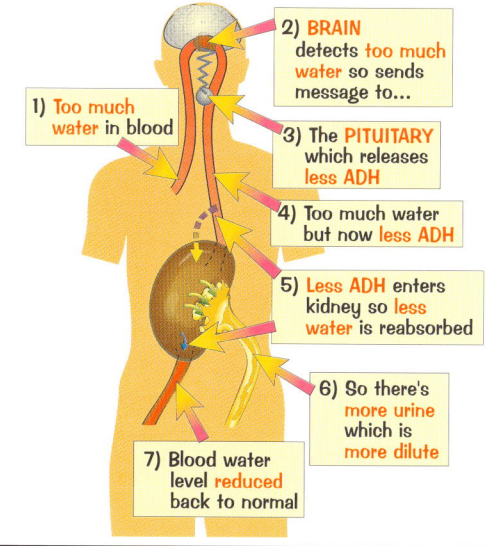

1) Too much water in blood
2) BRAIN detects too much water so sends message to...
3) The PITUITARY which releases less ADH
4) Too much water but now less ADH
5) Less ADH enters kidney so less water is reabsorbed
6) So there's more urine which is more dilute
7) Blood water level reduced back to normal

Phew — taking the mickey is much less complicated...

There's some tricky stuff on this page that's for sure. It's definitely a perfect candidate for the exciting mini-essay method. Learn the headings, then _cover the page_, write them down, and then _scribble a mini-essay_ for each one. Then look back and see what you missed. _Then try again_. And learn the diagrams, until you can repeat them too.

Causes of Disease

Disease

There are Two types of Microbes: Bacteria and Viruses

Microbes are organisms which get inside you and make you feel ill. There are two main types:

Bacteria are Very Small Living Cells

1) These are <u>very small cells</u>, (about 1/100th the size of your body cells), which reproduce rapidly inside your body.

2) They make you <u>feel ill</u> by doing <u>two</u> things:
   a) <u>damaging your cells</u>
   b) <u>producing toxins</u>.

3) Don't forget that some bacteria are <u>useful</u> if they're in the <u>right place</u>, like in your digestive system.

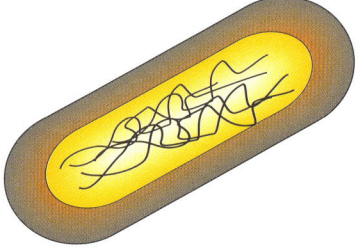

Bacteria are cells with no nucleus. The DNA is free in the cytoplasm

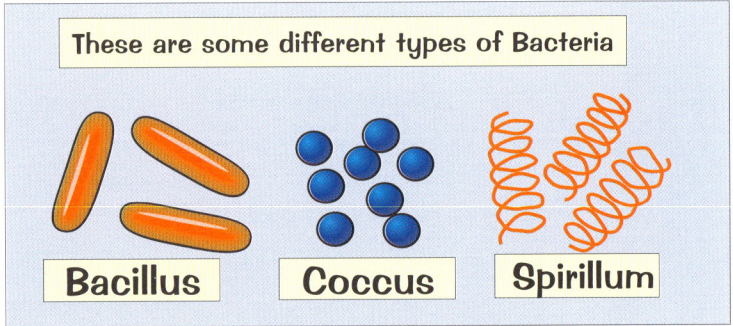

These are some different types of Bacteria

Bacillus   Coccus   Spirillum

Viruses are not cells — they're much smaller

1) These are <u>not cells</u>. They are <u>very very small</u>, about 1/100th the size of a bacterium.

2) They are no more than a <u>coat of protein</u> around a <u>DNA strand</u>.

3) They make you feel ill by <u>damaging your cells</u>.

4) They <u>replicate themselves</u> by invading the <u>nucleus</u> of a cell and using the <u>DNA</u> it contains to produce many <u>copies</u> of themselves.

5) The cell then <u>bursts</u>, releasing all the new viruses.

6) In this way they can reproduce <u>very quickly</u>.

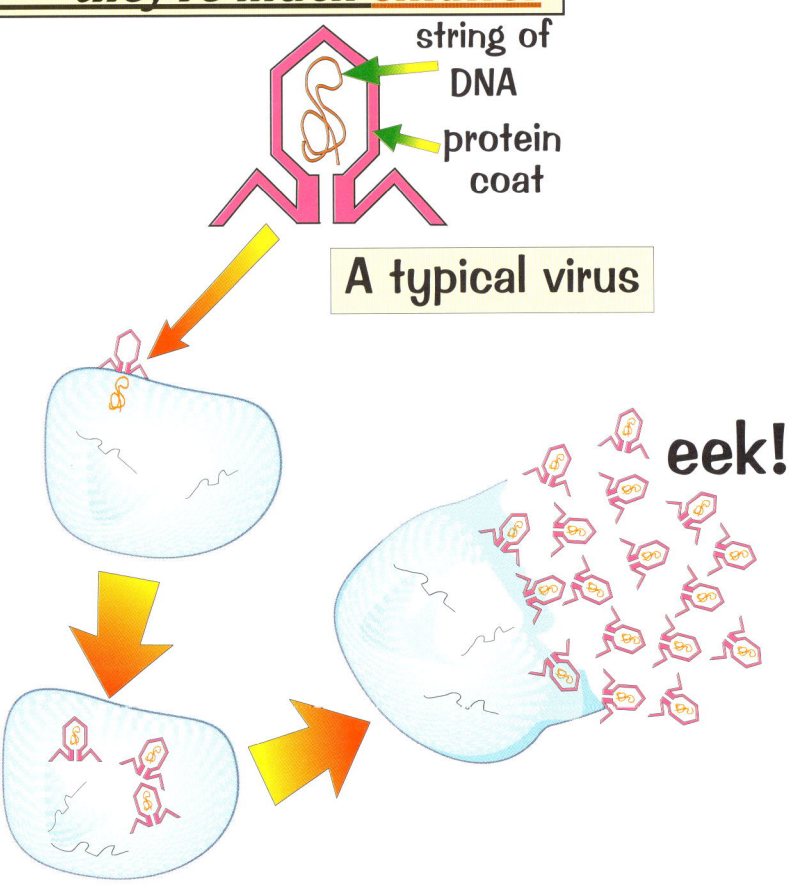

A typical virus

eek!

NEAB Syllabus — *Section Two — Humans as Organisms*

Disease in Humans

Disease

Diseases can be caused when *microbes* such as certain *bacteria* and *viruses* enter the body.

Disease is more likely to occur if large numbers of microbes enter the body as a result of *unhygienic conditions* or contact with *infected people*.

Five ways that microbes can enter our bodies

Microbes can enter our bodies in five ways, but we do have some *defences*.

1) Through the Skin and Eyes

Undamaged skin is a very effective barrier against microbes. If it gets damaged, the blood *clots* quickly to *seal cuts* and keep the microbes out. *Eyes* produce a chemical which *kills bacteria* on the surface of the eye.

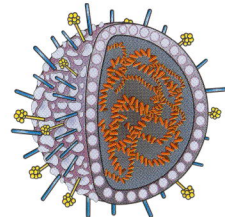

A horrid Flu Virus

2) Through the Digestive System

Contaminated food and *dirty water* allow microbes to enter your body. The stomach produces strong *hydrochloric acid* which *kills* most microbes which enter that way.

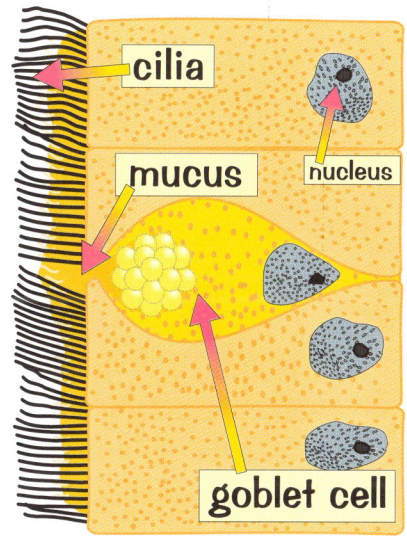

3) Through the Respiratory System

The whole *respiratory tract* (nasal passage, trachea and lungs) is lined with *mucus* and *cilia* which catch *dust* and *bacteria* before they reach the lungs.

4) Through the Reproductive System

Several diseases can be caught during sexual intercourse and our bodies have *few defences* against infection from such activities.

5) Through Vectors (e.g. mosquitos, fleas)

1) *Vectors* are *organisms* which *carry disease* from one person to another. For example the *mosquito* carries *malaria* from *person to person* when it stops to suck their *blood* (see P. 68 for some good news on the mosquito story).

2) Unfortunately we have *no natural protection* against insects *spitting* into our *bloodstream*.

3) *The black death*, which killed over *a quarter* of the entire population of *Europe* in the 1300's was carried from *person to person* by the *fleas* that live on *rats*. We don't tolerate rats any more, they're bad news.

(Apart from Adele's pet ones)

It's Grisly Stuff, but worth learning just the Same...

Two pages this time, and definitely 'mini-essay' material. There are three main sections, with several subsections. Do a *mini-essay* on each subsection and then *check* what you forgot.

Fighting Disease

Disease

Once microbes have entered our bodies they will _reproduce rapidly_ unless they are _destroyed_. Your '_immune system_' does just that, and _white blood cells_ are the most important part of it.

Your Immune System: White blood cells

They _travel around_ in your blood and _crawl into every part of you_, constantly _patrolling_ for microbes. When they come across an invading _microbe_ they have _three lines of attack_:

1) Consuming Them

White blood cells can _engulf_ foreign cells and _digest_ them.

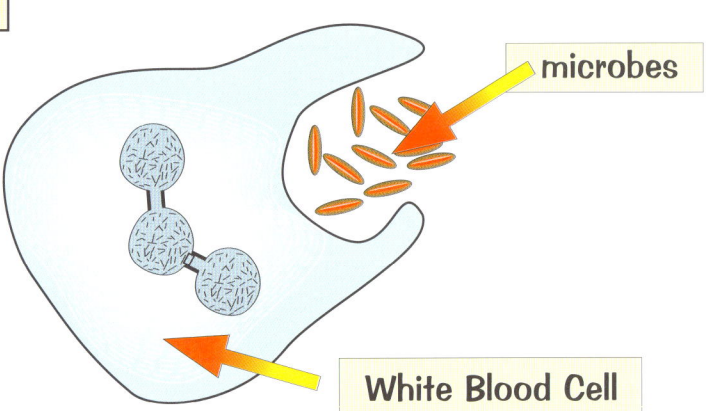

2) Producing Antibodies

When your white blood cells come across a _foreign cell_ they will _start to produce_ chemicals called _antibodies_ to kill the new invading cells.

The antibodies produced _rapidly_ and flow _all round the body_ to kill all _similar_ bacteria or viruses. If the same microbes are encountered in the future the same antibodies can be produced quickly making the person _immune_.

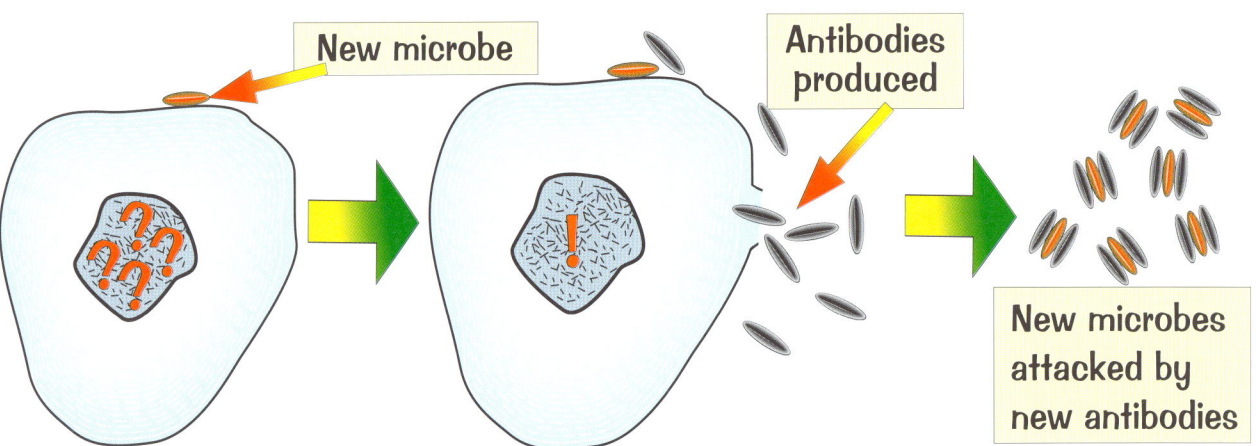

3) Producing Antitoxins

Antitoxins counter the effect of any _poisons_ (toxins) produced by the _invading bacteria_.

NEAB SYLLABUS

SECTION TWO — HUMANS AS ORGANISMS

Immunisation

Disease

Immunisation — producing antibodies beforehand

1) Once your *white cells* have produced *antibodies* to tackle a *new strain* of bacteria or virus you are said to have developed "*natural immunity*" to it.

2) That means if you get infected by the *same microbes* in future they'll be killed *immediately* by the *antibodies* you already have for them, and you *won't get ill*.

3) The trouble is when a *new* microbe appears, it takes your white cells *a few days* to produce the antibodies to deal with them and in that time you can get *very ill*.

4) There are *plenty of diseases* which can make you *very ill indeed* (e.g. polio, tetanus, measles) and only *immunisation* stops you getting them.

5) Immunisation involves injecting *dead microbes* into you. This causes your body to produce *antibodies* to them, even though they're dead. They can do no *harm* to you because they're dead.

6) If *live microbes of the same type* appeared *after that* however, they'd be *killed immediately* by the antibodies which you have already developed against them. Cool.

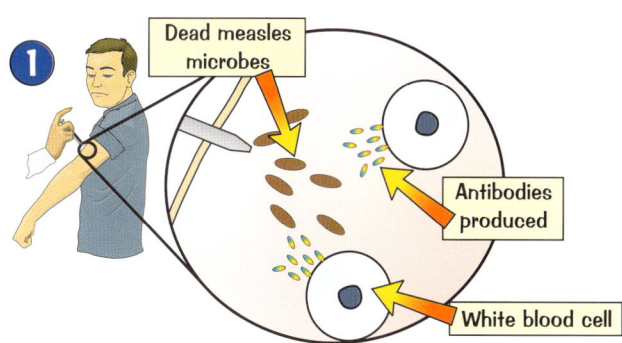

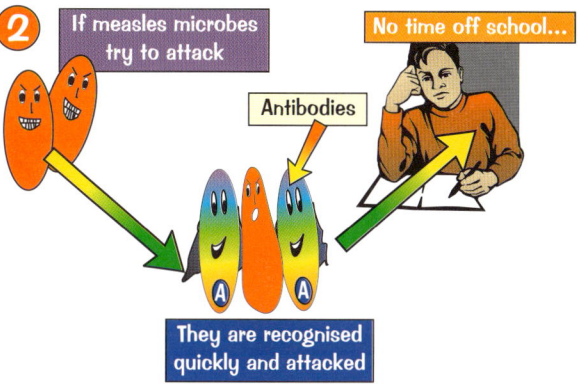

Antibiotics kill Bacteria but NOT Viruses

1) *Antibiotics* are *drugs* that kill *bacteria* without killing your own body cells.

2) They are *very useful* for clearing up infections that your body is having *trouble* with.

3) However they don't kill *viruses*. *Flu and colds* are caused by *viruses* and basically, *you're on your own*, pal.

4) There are *no drugs* to kill *viruses* and you just have to *wait* for your body to deal with it and *suffer* in the meantime.

5) Still, it's better than being bitten by a rat flea.

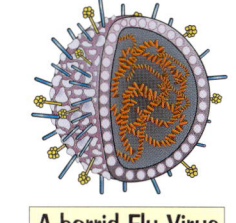

Don't let Revision make you sick — just learn and enjoy...

Don't let the big diagrams fool you — this stuff's complicated and needs careful learning. Make sure you *know all the details* of your body's natural immune system and the process of immunisation used to prevent disease. Make a list of *numbered points* for each page and keep learning them *till you know the lot*.

SECTION TWO — HUMANS AS ORGANISMS   NEAB SYLLABUS

Drugs

Drugs

1) Drugs are substances which alter the way the body works. Some drugs are useful of course, for example antibiotics such as penicillin. However there are many drugs which are _dangerous_ if misused, and many of them are _addictive_ or "habit-forming".
2) The loss of control and judgement caused by many drugs can easily lead to _death_ from various other causes e.g. choking on vomit, falling down stairs, passing under vehicles, etc.

Solvents

1) Solvents are found in a variety of "household" items e.g. glues, paints etc.
2) They are _dangerous_ and have many _damaging effects_ on your body and personality.
3) They cause hallucinations and adversely affect personality and behaviour.
4) They cause _damage_ to the _lungs_, _brain_ and _liver_.

Alcohol

1) The main effect of alcohol is to reduce the activity of the nervous system. The positive aspect of this is that it makes us feel less inhibited, and there's no doubt that alcohol in moderation helps people to socialise and relax with each other.
2) However, if you let alcohol take over, _it can wreck your life_. And it does. It wrecks a lot of people's lives. You've got to control it.
3) Once alcohol starts to take over someone's life there are many _harmful effects_:
    a) Alcohol is basically _poisonous_. Too much drinking will cause _severe damage_ to the _liver_ and the _brain_ leading to _liver disease_ and a noticeable _drop_ in brain function.
    b) Too much alcohol _impairs judgement_ which can cause accidents, and it can also severely affect the person's work and home life.
    c) _Serious dependency on alcohol_ can eventually lead to _loss of job_, _loss of income_ and the start of a _severe downward spiral_.

Smoking Tobacco

Smoking is no good to anyone. It doesn't have any positive social aspects and is _without any doubt at all a very serious cause of ill health_.

And you'll notice that smokers are _no happier_ than non-smokers, _even when they're smoking_. What may start off as something "different" to do, rapidly becomes something they _have_ to do, just to feel OK. But non-smokers feel just as OK _without_ spending £20 or more each week and _wrecking their health_ into the bargain.

Make sure you learn what tobacco smoke does inside your body:
1) It _coats_ the _inside of your lungs_ with tar so they become _hideously inefficient_.
2) It covers the cilia in _tar_ preventing them from getting bacteria out of your lungs.
3) It causes _disease_ of the _heart_ and _blood vessels_, leading to _heart attacks_ and _strokes_.
4) It causes _lung cancer_. Out of every _ten_ lung cancer patients, _nine_ of them smoke.
5) It causes _severe_ loss of lung function leading to diseases like _emphysema_ and _bronchitis_, in which the inside of the lungs is basically _wrecked_. People with severe bronchitis can't manage even a brisk walk, because their lungs can't get enough oxygen into the blood. It eventually _kills_ over _20,000 people_ in Britain every year.
6) But this is the best bit. The effect of the nicotine is _negligible_ — other than to make you _addicted_ to it. It doesn't make you high — just _dependent_. Great. Fantastic.

Learn the Numbered Points for your Exam...

It's the disease aspects they concentrate on most in the Exams. Learn the rest for a nice life.

NEAB Syllabus — SECTION TWO — HUMANS AS ORGANISMS

Revision Summary for Section Two

Phew, there's a lot of stuff to learn in Section Two. And it's all that grisly "open heart surgery" type stuff too, with all those gory diagrams. Mind you, it's all fairly straightforward and factual — you know, nothing difficult to understand, just lots of facts to learn. And lots of gory diagrams. You know the big plan with these questions though. Keep practising till you can whizz them all off without a moment's hesitation on any of them. It's a nice trick if you can do it.

1) Sketch the diagram below adding the names for parts A to G.

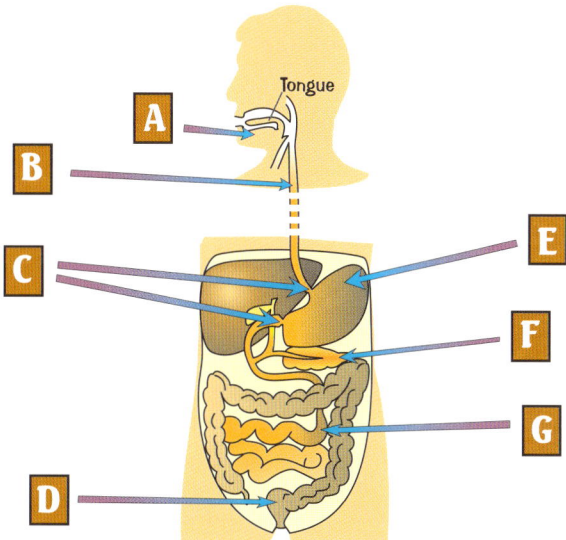

2) Add a further two labels to your diagram.
3) Write down at least two details for each of the labelled parts.
4) What *exactly* do enzymes do in the digestive system?
5) List the three main digestive enzymes, which foods they act on, and what they produce.
6) What *two* things does bile do? Where is it produced? Where does it enter the system?
7) Write down the seven types of nutrient needed in a balanced diet.
8) Say what kind of foods each one is found in, and what the nutrient is needed for.
9) Draw a diagram of the human circulatory system: heart, lungs, arteries, veins, etc.
10) Explain why it is a *double* circulatory system, and describe the pressure and oxygen content of the blood in each bit. What are the big words for saying if the blood has oxygen in or not?
11) Draw a full diagram of the heart with all the labels. Explain how the two halves differ.
12) How do ventricles and atria compare, and why? What are the valves for?
13) Describe briefly with diagrams the three stages of the pumping cycle for the heart.
14) Sketch an artery, a capillary, and a vein, with labels, and explain the features of all three.
15) Sketch a red blood cell and a white blood cell and give five details about each.
16) Sketch some blood plasma. List all the things that are carried in the plasma (around 10).
17) Sketch some platelets. What do they do all day?
18) Draw a diagram of the thorax, showing all the breathing equipment.
19) Describe what happens during breathing in and breathing out. Be sure to give all the details.
20) Where are alveoli found? How big are they and what are they for? Give four features.
21) Explain what happens to oxygen and carbon dioxide, both at alveoli and at body cells.
22) What is respiration? Give a proper definition.
23) What is "aerobic respiration"? Give the word equation for it.
24) What is "anaerobic respiration"? Give the word equation for what happens in our bodies.
25) Explain about fitness and the oxygen debt.

(continued over...)

Revision Summary for Section Two (continued)

Section Two's got all sorts of grisly bits and bobs in it. And some of it can be really quite hard to understand too. But it's all worth points in the Exam, and what do points mean? Prizes! These questions are designed to test what you know. They're pretty tough I grant you, but they really are the best way of revising. Keep trying these questions any time you feel like it, and for any you can't do, look back in Section Two and learn the answer to it for next time.

26) Draw a diagram showing the main parts of the nervous system.
27) List the five sense organs and say what kind of receptors each one has.
28) What are effectors? What two things constitute the central nervous system?
29) What are the three types of neuron? Draw a detailed diagram of a typical neuron.
30) Describe how a reflex arc works and why it's a good thing. Explain how a synapse works.
31) Copy this diagram of an eye and complete all the labels. Add brief details to the labelled parts.
32) Describe how the eye adjusts to focus on near and distant objects.

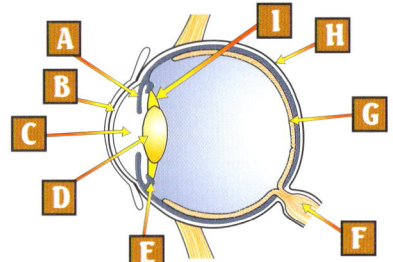

33) Draw a diagram of the body and label the five places where hormones are produced. Give details of what each hormones does.
34) Give the proper definition of hormones. What is an endocrine gland?
35) Explain what happens with insulin when the blood sugar is too high and when it is too low.
36) Draw diagrams to illustrate exactly what goes on in both cases.
37) What happens in diabetes? What are the two forms of treatment? How do they compare?
38) What are the drawbacks of taking: a) fertility drugs b) contraceptive drugs?
39) What are the three main hormones involved in the menstrual cycle and where do they originate? Draw a diagram showing exactly what these hormones do.
40) Give full details of which hormones are used: a) to promote fertility b) in "The Pill".
41) What is the proper definition for homeostasis? What are the six bodily levels involved?
42) Draw a diagram of the body showing the eight organs involved in homeostasis.
43) Say exactly what each of these organs does to help.
44) How does your skin help you to stay at a constant temperature?
45) What temperature do our bodily enzymes like?
46) Draw diagrams showing the three things the skin does when we're a) too hot b) too cold.
47) What is the basic function of the kidneys? What *three* particular things do they deal with?
48) Explain in detail exactly what the kidney does in relation to each of these three things.
49) Explain in detail the three stages of filtration in the kidneys.
50) Draw diagrams to explain how ADH is involved in regulating the water content of the blood.
51) What are the two types of microbe? How big are they compared to a human cell?
52) How exactly do bacteria make you feel ill? Sketch three common bacteria.
53) What do viruses do inside you to reproduce? Illustrate with sketches.
54) What are the five ways that microbes can enter our bodies?
55) Give details of the defences we have against these five methods of entry.
56) What is meant by your "immune system"? What is the most important part of it?
57) List the three ways that white blood cells deal with invading microbes.
58) Give full details of the process of immunisation. How does it work?
59) What are antibiotics? What will they work on and what will they not work on?
60) Explain the dangers of drinking alcohol. Explain why smoking is just *so cool* — not.
61) List in detail all five major health problems that result from smoking.

Green Plants as Organisms

Basic Plant Structure

Plant Nutrition

You have to know all these parts of the plant and what they do:

The Five Different Bits of a Plant all do Different Jobs

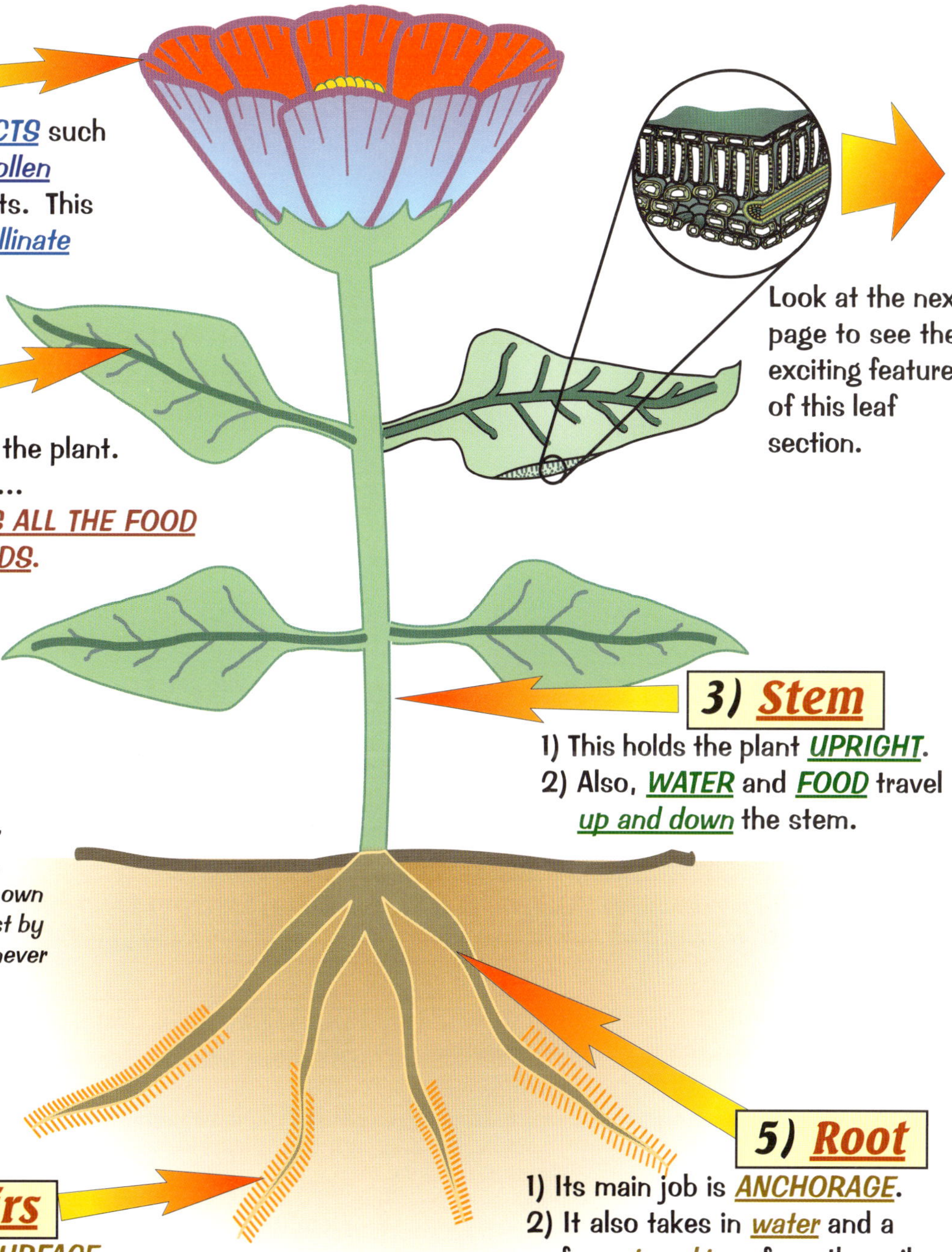

1) Flower

THIS ATTRACTS INSECTS such as bees which carry pollen between different plants. This allows the plants to pollinate and reproduce.

Look at the next page to see the exciting features of this leaf section.

2) Leaf

It produces FOOD for the plant. I'll say it again, listen....
THE LEAF PRODUCES ALL THE FOOD THAT THE PLANT NEEDS.

Plants do not take food from the soil. Plants make all their own food in their leaves using PHOTOSYNTHESIS.

(That's a bit of a shocker when you think about it. Imagine making all your own food under your skin just by lying in the sun — and never having to eat at all!)

3) Stem

1) This holds the plant UPRIGHT.
2) Also, WATER and FOOD travel up and down the stem.

4) Root hairs

These give A BIG SURFACE AREA to absorb water and ions from the soil.

5) Root

1) Its main job is ANCHORAGE.
2) It also takes in water and a few mineral ions from the soil. But mostly just water.
REMEMBER, plants do NOT take 'food' in from the soil.

The Big Idea is to LEARN All That...

Everything on this page is there to be LEARNT because it's very likely to come up in your Exams. This is pretty basic stuff, but it can still catch you out if you don't learn it properly. For example: "What is the main function of the root?". Too many people answer that with "Taking food in from the soil" — Eeek! LEARN these facts. They all count. They're all worth marks in the Exam. Practise until you can sketch the diagram and scribble down ALL the details, *without looking back*.

SECTION THREE — GREEN PLANTS AS ORGANISMS   NEAB SYLLABUS

Photosynthesis

Plant Nutrition

Photosynthesis Produces Glucose from Sunlight

1) _Photosynthesis_ is the process that produces _'food'_ in plants. The 'food' it produces is _glucose_.
2) Photosynthesis takes place in the _leaves_ of all _green plants_ — this is what leaves are for.

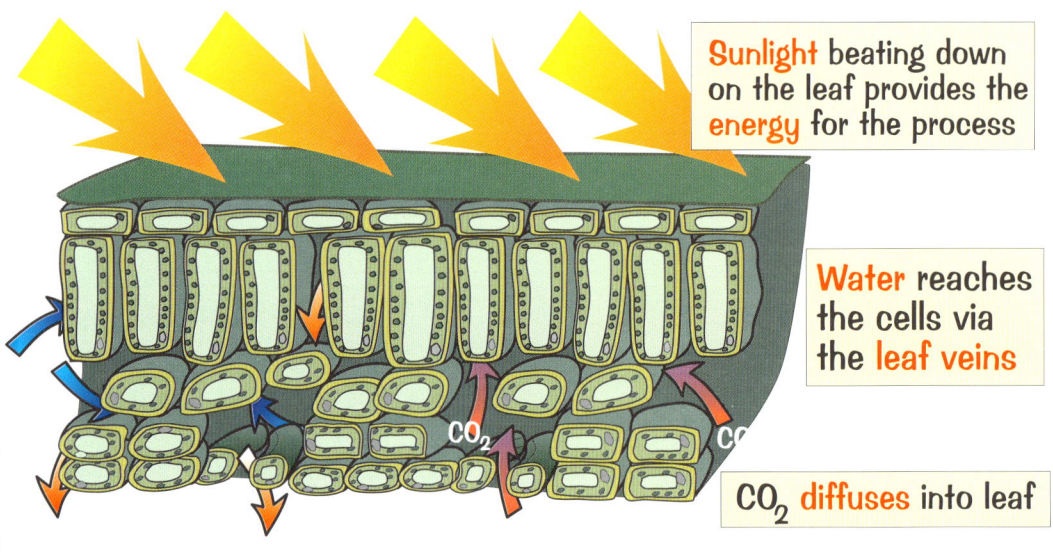

Sunlight beating down on the leaf provides the energy for the process

Water reaches the cells via the leaf veins

CO_2 diffuses into leaf

THREE FEATURES:
1) Leaves are _thin_ and _flat_ to provide a _big surface area_ to catch _lots_ of sunlight.
2) The _palisade_ cells are _near the top_ of the leaf and are packed with _chloroplasts_.
3) _Guard cells_ control the movement of _gases_ into and out of the leaf.

Learn the Equation for Photosynthesis:

$$\text{Carbon dioxide} + \text{Water} \xrightarrow[\text{chlorophyll}]{\text{SUNLIGHT}} \text{glucose} + \text{oxygen}$$

Four Things are Needed for Photosynthesis to Happen:

1) Light Usually from the _SUN_.

2) Chlorophyll The _green substance_ which is found in _chloroplasts_ and which makes leaves look _green_.

This is the 'magic' stuff that makes it all happen. Chlorophyll _absorbs the energy in sunlight_ and uses it to combine CO_2 and _WATER_ to produce _GLUCOSE_. Oxygen is simply a by-product.

3) Carbon dioxide Enters the leaf from the _AIR_ around.

4) Water Comes _FROM THE SOIL_, up the stem and into the leaf.

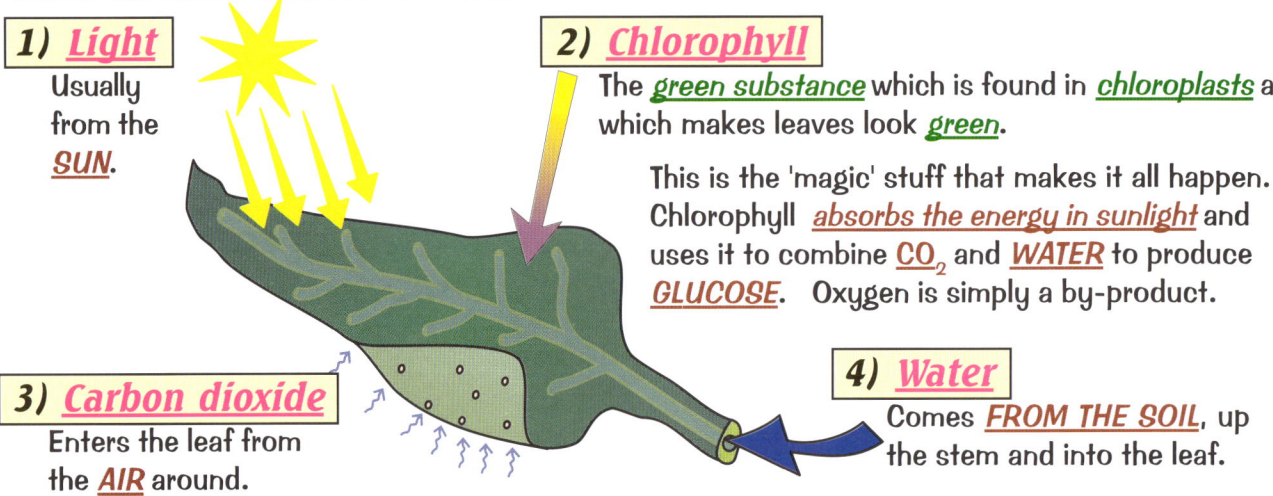

Live and Learn...

What you've got to do now is learn everything on this page. Photosynthesis is a "dead cert" for the Exams. On this page you've got two diagrams, two points about photosynthesis and the equation, and then the four necessary conditions. Just _keep learning them_ until you can _cover the page_ and write them all down _from memory_. Only then will you really _know it all_.

NEAB Syllabus — SECTION THREE — GREEN PLANTS AS ORGANISMS

The Rate of Photosynthesis

Plant Nutrition

The RATE of photosynthesis is affected by THREE FACTORS:

1) THE AMOUNT OF LIGHT

The chlorophyll uses light energy to perform photosynthesis. It can only do it as fast as the light energy is arriving. Chlorophyll actually only absorbs the red and blue ends of the visible light spectrum, but not the green light in the middle, which is reflected back. This is why the plant looks green.

2) THE AMOUNT OF CARBON DIOXIDE

CO_2 and water are the raw materials. Water is never really in short supply in a plant but only 0.03% of the air around is CO_2 so it's actually pretty scarce as far as plants are concerned.

3) THE TEMPERATURE

Chlorophyll is like an ENZYME so it works best when it's warm but not too hot. The rate of photosynthesis depends on how 'happy' the chlorophyll enzyme is: WARM but not too hot.

Three Important Graphs For Rate of Photosynthesis

At any given time one or other of the above three factors will be the limiting factor which is keeping the photosynthesis down at the rate it is.

1) Not Enough LIGHT Slows Down the Rate of Photosynthesis

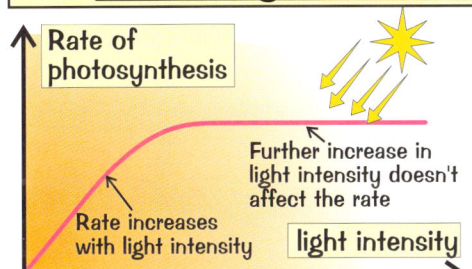

1) As the light level is raised, the rate of photosynthesis increases steadily but only up to a certain point.
2) Beyond that, it won't make any difference because then it'll be either the temperature or the CO_2 level which is the limiting factor.

2) Too Little CARBON DIOXIDE also Slows it Down

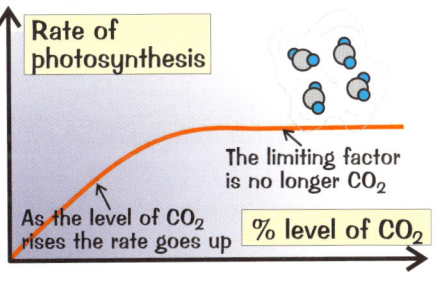

1) As with light intensity the amount of CO_2 will only increase the rate of photosynthesis up to a point. After this the graph flattens out showing that CO_2 is no longer the limiting factor.
2) As long as light and CO_2 are in plentiful supply then the factor limiting photosynthesis must be temperature.

3) The TEMPERATURE has to be Just Right

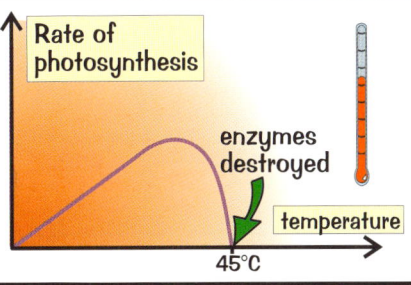

1) Note that you can't really have too much light or CO_2. The temperature however must not get too high or it destroys the chlorophyll enzymes.
2) This happens at about 45°C (which is pretty hot for outdoors, though greenhouses can get that hot if you're not careful).
3) Usually, though, if the temperature is the limiting factor it's because it's too low, and things need warming up a bit.

Revision — life isn't all fun and sunshine...

There are three limiting factors, a graph for each and an explanation of why the graphs level off or stop abruptly. Cover the page and practise recalling all these details, until you can do it.

SECTION THREE — GREEN PLANTS AS ORGANISMS

How Plants Use The Glucose

Plant Nutrition

1) Plants manufacture _glucose_ in their _leaves_.
2) They then use some of the glucose initially for _respiration_.
3) This _releases energy_ which enables them to _convert_ the rest of the glucose into various _other useful substances_ which they can use to _build new cells_ and _grow_.
4) To produce some of these substances they also need to _gather_ a few _minerals_ from the soil.

For Respiration ①

Making Fruits ②
GLUCOSE is turned into SUCROSE for storing in FRUITS. Fruits deliberately _taste nice_ so that animals will eat them and so _spread the seeds_ all over the place.

Stored in Seeds ③
GLUCOSE is turned into LIPIDS (fats and oils) for storing in SEEDS. Sunflower seeds, for example, contain a lot of oil — we get _cooking oil_ and _margarine_ from them.

⑤ For Transport
The ENERGY from GLUCOSE is also needed to _transport substances_ around the plant and for ACTIVE UPTAKE of _minerals_ in the roots.

④ Making Cell walls
GLUCOSE is converted into CELLULOSE for making _cell walls_, especially in a rapidly growing plant.

⑦ Making Proteins
GLUCOSE is combined with NITRATES (collected from the soil) to make AMINO ACIDS, which are then made into PROTEINS.

⑥ Stored as Starch
Glucose is turned into _starch_ and _stored_ in roots, stems and leaves, ready for use when photosynthesis isn't happening, like in the _winter_.
STARCH is INSOLUBLE which makes it much _better_ for _storing_, because it doesn't bloat the storage cells by _osmosis_ like glucose would.

Potato and carrot plants store a lot of starch in their roots over the winter to enable a new plant to grow from it the following spring. We eat the swollen roots!

"Sugar it", that's what I say...

There are seven things that plants do with glucose. Can you spot them? If so, _learn them_, _cover the page_, and then display your new-found knowledge. In other words, sketch out the diagram and _scribble down_ the seven ways that plants use glucose, including all the extra details.

NEAB SYLLABUS — SECTION THREE — GREEN PLANTS AS ORGANISMS

Minerals For Healthy Growth

Plant Nutrition

For _healthy growth_ plants need these three really important mineral ions which they can only obtain from the _soil_ through their _roots_:

The Three Essential Minerals

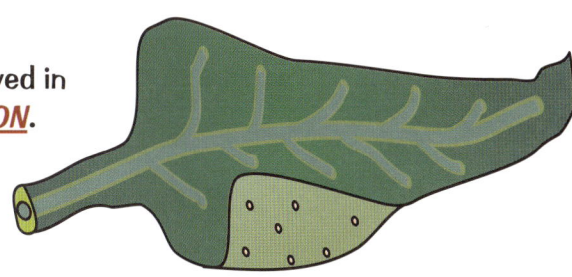

1) Nitrates
— for making AMINO ACIDS and for the "synthesis" (making) of PROTEINS.

2) Phosphates
— have an important role in reactions involved in PHOTOSYNTHESIS and RESPIRATION.

3) Potassium
— helps the ENZYMES involved in PHOTOSYNTHESIS and RESPIRATION to work.

Lack of These Nutrients Causes Deficiency Symptoms:

1) Lack of Nitrates
— STUNTED GROWTH and YELLOW OLDER LEAVES.

2) Lack of Phosphates
— POOR ROOT GROWTH and PURPLE YOUNGER LEAVES.

3) Lack of Potassium
— YELLOW LEAVES with DEAD SPOTS.

The Perils of Monoculture

1) _Monoculture_ is where JUST ONE TYPE OF CROP is grown in the same field _year after year_.
2) This causes the soil to become _deficient_ in the _minerals_ which that particular plant uses lots of.
3) _Deficiency_ of just _one mineral_ is enough to cause _poor growth_ and _reduced yield_.
4) This soon results in poor crops unless _fertiliser_ is added to _replenish_ the depleted minerals.

Just relax and soak up the information...

Very straightforward learning here. Two nice big clear sections with all the important bits highlighted in colour as usual. You should be able to _cover this page_ and _scribble_ virtually the whole thing down again with very little bother. _Learn and enjoy._

SECTION THREE — GREEN PLANTS AS ORGANISMS   NEAB SYLLABUS

Growth Hormones in Plants

Plant Hormones

Auxins are Plant Growth Hormones

1) Auxins are hormones which control growth at the tips of shoots and roots.
2) Auxin is produced in the tips and diffuses backwards to stimulate the cell elongation process which occurs in the cells just behind the tips.
3) If the tip of a shoot is removed, no auxin will be available and the shoot may stop growing.

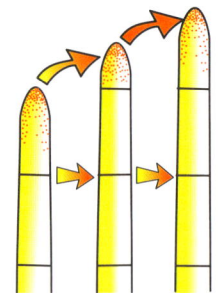

Auxins Change The Direction of Root and Shoot Growth

You'll note below that extra auxin promotes growth in the shoot but actually inhibits growth in the root — but also note that this produces the desired result in both cases.

1) Shoots bend towards the light

1) When a shoot tip is exposed to light, it provides more auxin on the side that is in the shade than the side which is in the light.
2) This causes the shoot to grow faster on the shaded side and it bends towards the light.

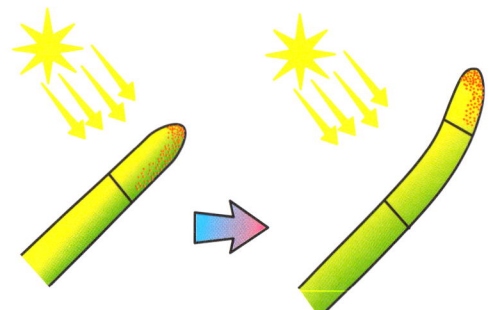

2) Shoots bend away from Gravity

1) When a shoot finds itself growing sideways, the gravity produces an unequal distribution of auxin in the tip, with more auxin on the lower side.
2) This causes the lower side to grow faster, thus bending the shoot upwards.

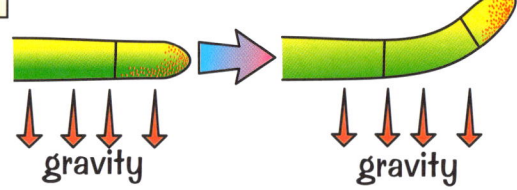

3) Roots bend towards Gravity

1) A root growing sideways will experience the same redistribution of auxin to the lower side.
2) But in a root the extra auxin actually inhibits growth, causing it to bend downwards instead.

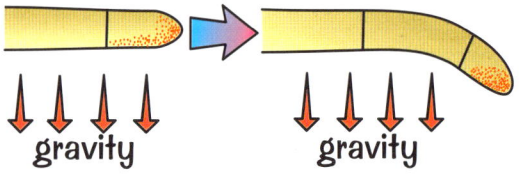

4) Roots bend towards Moisture

1) An uneven degree of moisture either side of a root will cause more auxin to appear on the side with more moisture.
2) This inhibits growth on that side, causing the root to grow in that direction, towards the moisture.

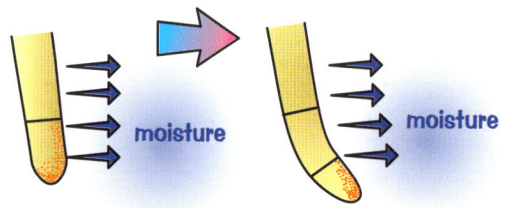

Just A Few Tips for Your Revision...

An easy page to learn. Just three points on auxins, together with a diagram, and then four ways that shoots and roots change direction, with a diagram for each. You just have to learn it. Then cover the page and scribble down the main points from memory. Then try again, and again...

Commercial Use of Hormones

Plant Hormones

Plant hormones have a lot of uses in the _food growing business_.

1) Producing Seedless Fruit

1) Fruits normally only grow on plants which have been _pollinated by insects_, with the inevitable _seeds_ in the middle of the fruit. If the plant _doesn't_ get pollinated, the fruits and seeds _don't grow_.
2) However, if _growth hormones_ are applied to _unpollinated flowers_ the _fruits will grow_ but the _seeds won't_!
3) This is great. Seedless satsumas and seedless grapes are just _so much nicer_ than the 'natural' ones full of pips!

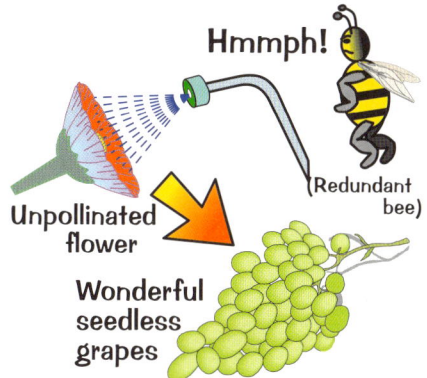

2) Controlling the Ripening of Fruit

1) The _ripening_ of fruits can be controlled either while they are _still on the plant_, or during _transport_ to the shops.
2) This allows the fruit to be picked while it's still _unripe_ (and therefore firmer and _less easily damaged_).
3) It can then be sprayed with _ripening hormone_ and it will ripen _on the way_ to the supermarket to be perfect just as it reaches the shelves.

3) Growing from Cuttings with Rooting Compound

1) A _cutting_ is part of a plant that has been _cut off it_, like the end of a branch with a few leaves on it.
2) Normally, if you stick cuttings in the soil they _won't grow_, but if you add _rooting compound_, which is a plant _growth hormone_, they will produce roots rapidly and start growing as _new plants_.
3) This enables growers to produce lots of _clones_ (exact copies) of a really good plant _very quickly_.

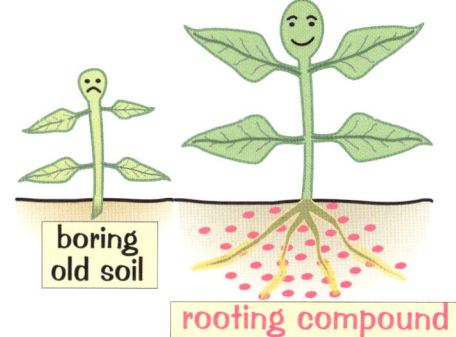

4) Killing Weeds

1) Most weeds growing in fields of crops or in a lawn are _broad-leaved_, in contrast to grass which has very _narrow leaves_.
2) _Selective weedkillers_ have been developed from _plant growth hormones_ which only affects the broad-leaved plants.
3) They totally _disrupt_ their normal _growth patterns_, which soon _kills_ them, whilst leaving the grass untouched.

Remember, serious learning always bears fruit...

Another blissfully easy page. Just make sure you learn enough about each bit to answer a 3 mark Exam question on it (that means being able to make 3 valid points). As usual the sections are split into numbered points to help you remember them. They've all got three points to learn. _So learn them_. Then _cover the page_ and _scribble down_ the 3 points for each. And tell me this: — if you can't do it now, what makes you think it'll all suddenly _"come back to you"_ in the Exam?

SECTION THREE — GREEN PLANTS AS ORGANISMS — NEAB SYLLABUS

The Transpiration Stream

Transport and Water Relations

Transpiration is the loss of water from the Plant

1) It's caused by the *evaporation* of water from *inside* the *leaves*. Most of the action involves the *stomata* shown on the following page.
2) This creates a *slight shortage* of water in the leaf which *draws more water up* from the rest of the plant which *in turn* draws more up from the *roots*.
3) It has *two beneficial effects*:   a) it *transports minerals* from the soil   b) it *cools* the plant.

water evaporates from the leaves

water soaks into the roots

The uptake of WATER and MINERALS happens almost entirely at the ROOT HAIRS (see diagram on P. 47).

Four factors which affect it

The *rate of transpiration* is affected by *four things*:
 1) Amount of *light*
 2) *Temperature*
 3) Amount of *air movement*
 4) *Humidity* of the surrounding air

It's surely obvious that the *biggest* rate of transpiration occurs in *hot*, *dry*, *windy*, *sunny* conditions
   i.e. perfect clothes-drying weather.

By contrast a *cool*, *cloudy*, *muggy*, *miserable day* with *no wind* will produce *minimum transpiration*.

This constant stream of water has the advantage of transporting *vital minerals* from the *SOIL* into the roots and then all around the plant.

Leaves Help to Limit Transpiration

Waxy Cuticle (Waterproof layer)

Guard Cell
Stomatal pore
Leaf Vein (containing xylem and phloem tubes)

The leaves on most plants have a *waxy top layer* to *limit transpiration*.
As you'd expect, plants living in *dryer* conditions have a *thicker layer* of wax.

It helps if you're quick on the uptake...

There's quite a lot of information on this page. You could try learning the numbered points, but you'll find a better plan is to do a *"mini-essay"* on transpiration and write down everything you can think of. Then look back to see what you've forgotten. Then do it again! *Till you get it all*.

The Cells' Role in Transpiration

Transport and Water Relations

Root Hair cell

1) The cells on plant roots grow into long "_hairs_" which stick out into the soil.
2) This gives the plant a _big surface area_ for absorbing _water and minerals_ from the soil.
3) _Water_ is taken in almost entirely at the root hairs.
4) _Minerals_ are also taken in at the root hairs.
5) However this uptake of minerals is against the concentration gradient, so it needs "_active uptake_" to make it happen.

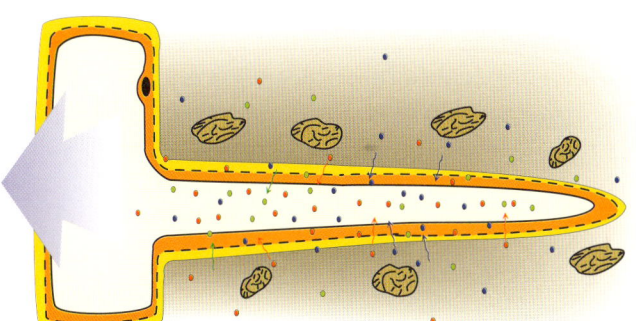

Turgor Pressure Supports Plant Tissues

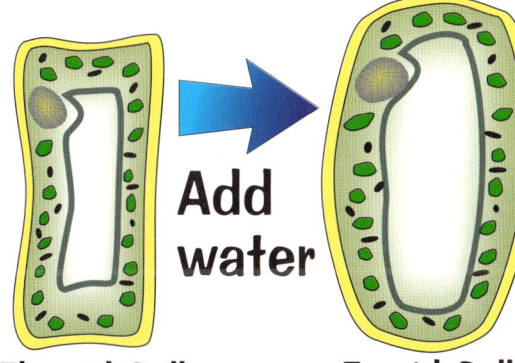

Flaccid Cell → Add water → Turgid Cell

1) When a plant is _well watered_, all its cells will draw water into themselves by _osmosis_ and become _turgid_.
2) The contents of the cell start to push against the _cell wall_, kind of like a balloon in a shoebox, and thereby give _support_ to the plant tissues.
3) _Leaves_ are entirely supported by this _turgor pressure_.

We know this because if there's no water in the soil, a plant starts to _wilt_ and the leaves _droop_. This is because the cells start to lose water and thus lose their turgor pressure.

Stomata are Pores which Open and Close Automatically

1) _Stomata_ close _automatically_ when supplies of water from the roots start to _dry up_.
2) The _guard cells_ control this. When water is _scarce_, they become _flaccid_, and they change shape, which _closes_ the stomatal pores.
3) This _prevents_ any more _water_ being _lost_, but also stops CO_2 getting in, so the photosynthesis stops as well.

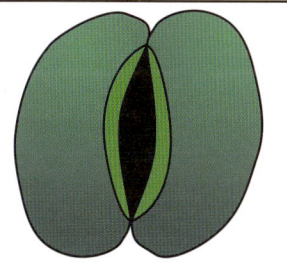
Cells TURGID, pore OPENS

Cells FLACCID, pore CLOSES

Limiting water loss is especially important in _younger plants_ as water pressure is their main method of _support_.

Spend some time poring over these facts...

Three spiffing diagrams and a few simple features. What could be easier? Check the clock and give yourself five minutes of intense active learning to see how much you can learn. "_Intense active learning_" means _covering the page_ and _scribbling down_ the details, but don't take 5 minutes drawing out a neat diagram of a root hair — that's just a waste of precious time.

SECTION THREE — GREEN PLANTS AS ORGANISMS   NEAB SYLLABUS

Transport Systems in Plants

Transport and Water Relations

Plants need to transport various things around inside themselves. They have tubes for it.

Phloem and Xylem Vessels Transport Different Things

1) Flowering plants have _two_ separate sets of _tubes_ for transporting stuff around the plant.
2) _Both_ sets of tubes go to _every part_ of the plant, but they are totally _separate_.
3) They usually run _alongside_ each other.

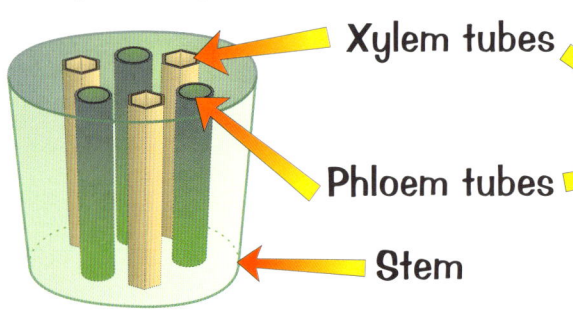

Xylem tubes — Phloem tubes — Stem

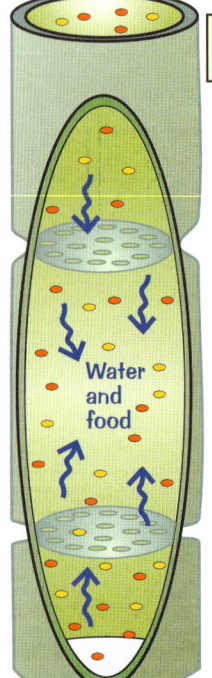

Phloem Tubes transport Food:

1) Made of _living cells_ with _perforated end-plates_ to allow stuff to flow through.
2) They transport _food_ made in the _leaves_ to _all other parts_ of the plant, in _both directions_.
3) They carry _sugars_, _fats_, _proteins_ etc. to _growing regions_ in _shoot tips_ and _root tips_ and to/from _storage organs_ in the _roots_.

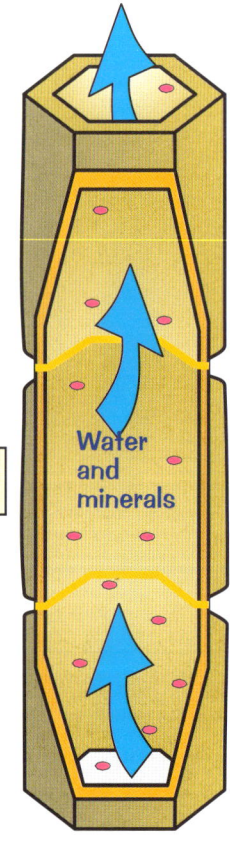

Xylem Tubes take water UP:

1) Made of _dead cells_ joined end to end with _no end walls_ between them.
2) The side walls are _strong and stiff_ and contain _lignin_. This gives the plant _support_.
3) They carry _water and minerals_ from the _roots_ up to the leaves in the transpiration stream.

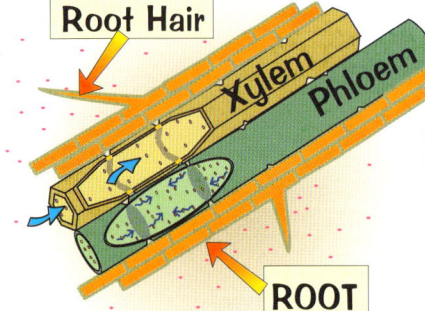

The Phloem and Xylem extend into the Roots

1) The _phloem_ carries _starch_ down to the _roots_ for _growth_ or for _storage_ and may later carry it _back up again_.
2) The _xylem_ carries _water and minerals_, (which are taken in by the roots), _up_ to the stem and into the leaves.

Well that seems to be about the top and bottom of it...

This is an easy page. There are important differences between xylem and phloem tubes. Make sure you know all the numbered points on this page, and the diagrams. Then cover the page and scribble it all down with detailed sketches of the diagrams. Then do it again, _until you get it all_.

NEAB Syllabus — SECTION THREE — GREEN PLANTS AS ORGANISMS

Revision Summary For Section Three

*Jeepers creepers. Well, it's a pretty short section, but it still all needs learning.
A quick way to do this is to make use of all the pictures — these are far easier to remember than just lists and lists of facts. Once you know the pictures it's fairly simple to tag on any extra info.
You'll soon find that simply drawing the picture will help you recall the rest. So even if the question doesn't ask for a picture it's still worth doing a quick sketch.
Same drill as usual with these questions — keep going till you know the lot.
Just remember to use pictures to help jog your memory.*

1) Sketch a typical plant and label the five important parts.
2) Explain exactly what each bit does.
3) What does photosynthesis do? Where does it do it?
4) Write down the word equation for photosynthesis.
5) Sketch a leaf and show the four things needed for photosynthesis.
6) What are the three variable quantities which affect the rate of photosynthesis?
7) Sketch a graph for each one and explain the shape.
8) Describe conditions where each of the three factors is in short supply.
9) Sketch a plant and label the seven ways that plants use glucose.
10) Give a couple of extra details for each of the seven uses.
11) List the three essential minerals needed for healthy plant growth, and what they're needed for.
12) What are symptoms of the plants below? What is each plant lacking?

13) What are the perils of monoculture?
14) What are auxins? Where are they produced?
15) Name the four ways that auxins affect roots and shoots.
16) Give full details for all four.
17) How are seedless grapes made?
18) Explain what rooting compound is used for.
19) How do hormonal weed killers work?
20) Name and describe one more commercial use of hormones
21) What is transpiration? What causes it? What benefits does it bring?
22) How do leaves help to limit transpiration? What does this mean for plants in drier climates?
23) What are the four factors which affect the rate of transpiration?
24) What is the root hair's role in transpiration? Explain the processes involved.
25) How are minerals absorbed by the roots?
26) What is turgor pressure? How does is come about and what use is it to plants?
27) Explain what stomata do and how they do it.
28) What are the two types of tubes in plants? Whereabouts are they found in plants?
29) List three features for both types of tube and sketch them both.
30) Sketch a root and say what goes on in the tubes inside it.

SECTION THREE — GREEN PLANTS AS ORGANISMS   NEAB SYLLABUS

Variation, Inheritance and Evolution

Variation in Plants and Animals — *Variation*

1) Young plants and animals obviously *resemble* their *parents*. In other words they show *similar characteristics* such as jagged leaves or perfect eyebrows.

2) However young animals and plants can also *differ* from their parents and each other.

3) These similarities and differences lead to *variation* within the same species.

4) The word "VARIATION" sounds far too fancy for its own good. All it means is how animals or plants of the same species *look or behave* slightly different from each other. You know, a bit *taller* or a bit *fatter* or a bit more *scary-to-look-at* etc.

There are *two* causes of variation: *Genetic Variation* and *Environmental Variation*.

Read on, and learn...

1) Genetic variation

You'll know this already.

1) *All animals* (including humans) are bound to be *slightly different* from each other because their *GENES* are slightly different.

2) Genes are the code inside all your cells which determine how your body turns out. We all end up with a slightly different set of genes.

3) The *exceptions* to that rule are *identical twins*, because their genes are *exactly the same*.

But even identical twins are never *completely identical* — and that's because of the other factor:

2) Environmental Variation *is shown up by* Twins

If you're not sure what "*environment*" means, think of it as "*upbringing*" instead — it's pretty much the same thing — how and where you were "brought up".

Since we know the *twins' genes* are *identical*, any differences between them *must* be caused by slight differences *in their environment* throughout their lives.

Twins give us a fairly good idea of how important the *two factors* (genes and environment) are, *compared to each other*, at least for animals — plants always show much *greater variation* due to differences in their environment than animals do, as explained below.

Environmental Variation in Plants is much Greater

PLANTS are *strongly affected* by:
1) *Temperature*
2) *Sunlight*
3) *Moisture level*
4) *Soil composition*

For example, plants may grow *twice as big* or *twice as fast* due to *fairly modest* changes in environment such as the amount of *sunlight* or *rainfall* they're getting, or how *warm* it is or what the *soil* is like.

A cat, on the other hand, born and bred in the North of Scotland, could be sent out to live in equatorial Africa and would show no significant changes — it would look the same, eat the same, and it would probably still puke up everywhere.

NEAB Syllabus — Section Four — Variation, Inheritance & Evolution

Variation in Plants and Animals

Variation

Environmental Variation in Animals

Stubborn cats notwithstanding...

In Exams they do like questions on *the* effects of *environment on animals*.

Typically, they'll ask you *which features* of a human or a pet *MIGHT be affected* by their environment (i.e. the way they were "brought up").

In fact, *almost every single aspect* of a human (or animal) will be affected by *upbringing* in some way, however small, and in fact it's considerably easier to list the very few factors that *aren't* affected by environment and these are they:

4 Animal Characteristics NOT affected at all by Environment:

1) *EYE COLOUR*.
2) *HAIR COLOUR* in most animals (but not humans where vanity plays a big part).
3) *INHERITED DISEASES* like haemophilia, cystic fibrosis, etc.
4) *BLOOD GROUP*.

And that's about it! So *learn those four* in case they ask you.

Combinations of Genetic and Environmental Variation

EVERYTHING ELSE is determined by *A MIXTURE* of *genetic* and *environmental* factors: *Body weight*, *height*, *skin colour*, *condition of teeth*, *academic or athletic prowess*, etc. etc.

The *tricky* bit is working out just *how significant* environmental factors are for all these other features.

For example...

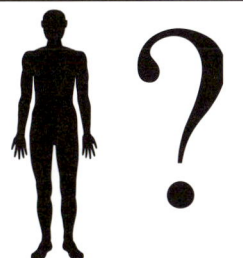

...imagine you got mixed up with another baby at the hospital and had grown up in a *totally different household* from your own. How different would you be now? It's not at all easy to tell how much of your *physique* and (more importantly) your *personality* are due to *genes* and how much to *upbringing* (*environment*). It's a big social issue, so it is.

Don't let Everything get to you — just learn the facts...

There are six sections on these two pages. After you think you've learnt it all, *cover the pages* and do a "*mini-essay*" on each of the six sections. Then *check back* and see what important points you missed. The coloured ink highlights the important bits.

Genetics: Too Many Fancy Words

Genetics and DNA

When it comes to *big fancy words* then *Biology* is the subject where it's all happening. And *genetics* is the topic that *REALLY* walks away with all the prizes.
It seems *hard to believe* that so many exceptionally cumbersome, excessively complicated and virtually unintelligible words can conceivably be necessary, or indeed be particularly desirable...

Here's a summary of all the fancy words used in *genetics* with an explanation of what they actually mean. It really does make a *big difference* if you *learn* these first. It's very difficult to understand *anything* in genetics if you don't actually know what half the words mean.

DNA — is the *molecule* which contains *genes*. It's shaped like a *double helix* (a spiral).

Chromosomes — are those funny *X-shaped* things that are found in the *cell nucleus*. The arms are made up of *very long coils of DNA*, so chromosomes also contain *genes*.

Gene — is a *section of DNA molecule*. It's also part of the *arm* of a chromosome.

Allele — is a *gene* too. When you have *two different versions* of the same gene you have to call them *alleles* instead of genes. (It *is* more sensible than it sounds.)

Higher Higher Higher

Dominant — this refers to an *allele* or *gene*. The dominant allele is the one which will *determine* the characteristic which appears. *It dominates the recessive allele* on the other chromosome.

Recessive — is the *allele* which does *not* usually affect how the organism turns out because it's *dominated* by the dominant allele (fairly obviously).

Homozygous — is an individual with *two alleles the same* for that particular gene, e.g. **HH** or **hh**.

Heterozygous — is an individual with *two alleles different* for that particular gene, e.g. **Hh**.

Meiosis — is the process of *cell division* which *creates sperm or egg cells*. Meiosis only happens in the *ovaries* or the *testes*.

Mitosis — is the process of *cell division* where one cell splits into *two identical cells*.

Gamete — is either a *sperm cell* or an *egg cell*.
All *gametes* have half the number of chromosomes of a body cell.

Zygote — is the delightful name given to each newly-formed human life, just after the (equally delightfully-named) *gametes fuse together* at fertilisation.

You'd think they could have come up with some slightly prettier names, as would befit this most awesome and wonderful moment, really. Your whole life, that great voyage of discovery and wonder, of emotion and reason, of conscience and consciousness, begins with that fateful and magical moment when...
..."two GAMETES fuse to form a ZYGOTE"...   Ahh, what poetry...

Too many fancy words, but you still gotta learn 'em...

Practise by covering up the right hand side of the page and scribbling down a description for each word. That's nice and easy. Just keep looking back and practising *till you can do them all*.

NEAB Syllabus   Section Four — Variation, Inheritance & Evolution

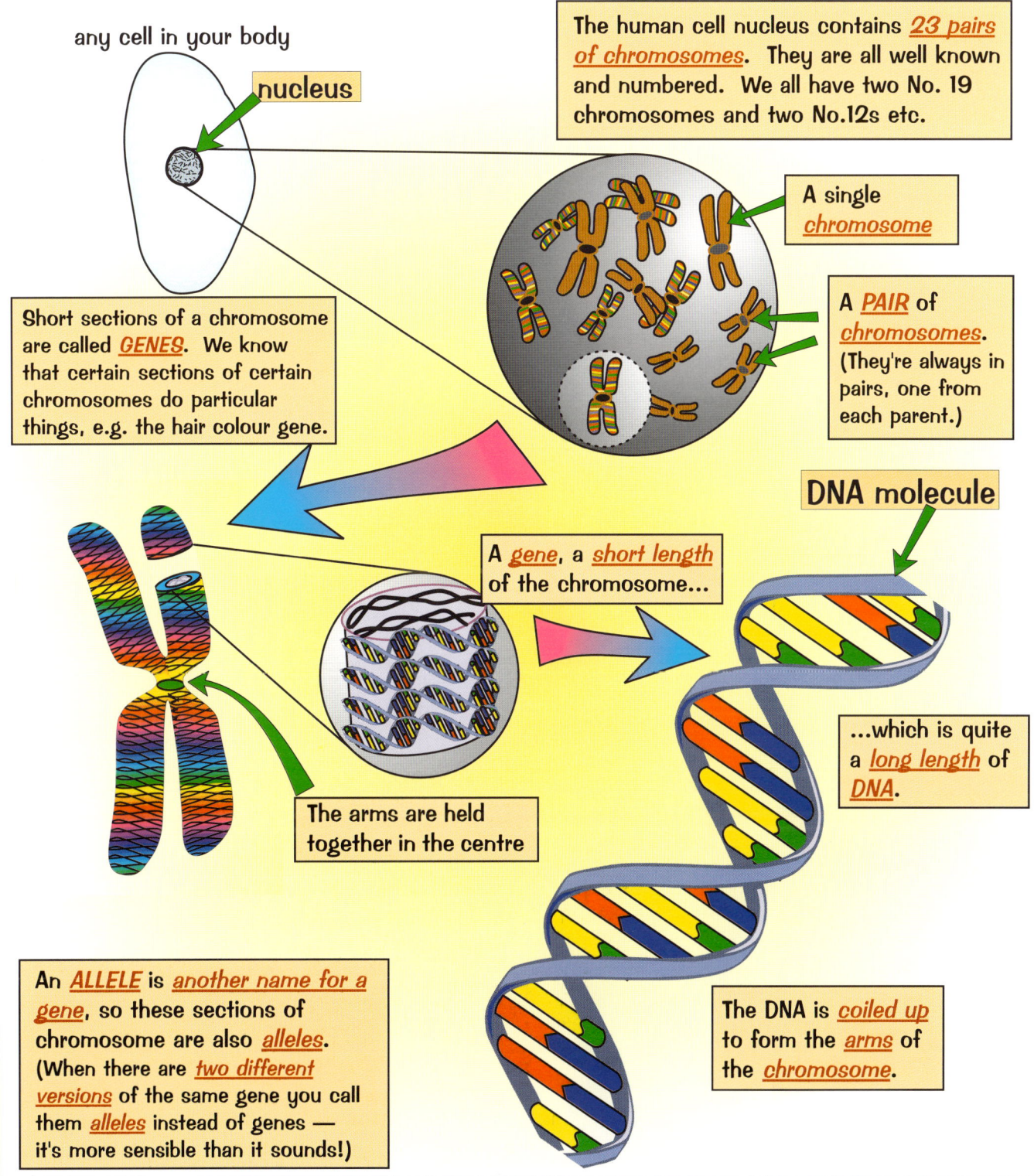

Ordinary Cell Division: Mitosis

Cell Division

"MITOSIS is when a cell reproduces itself ASEXUALLY by splitting to form two identical offspring that are called clones."

The really riveting part of the whole process is how the chromosomes split inside the cell. Learn and enjoy...

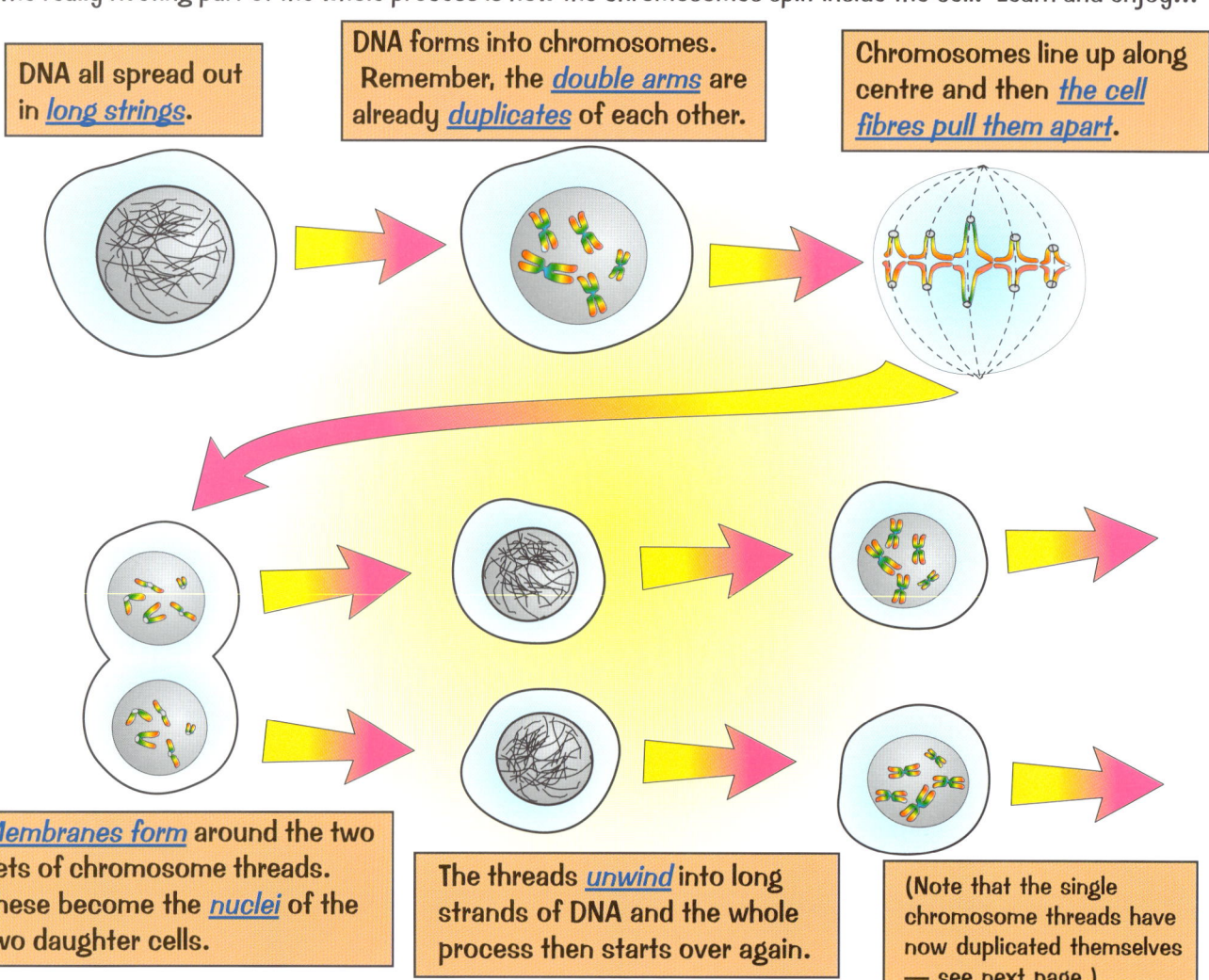

DNA all spread out in long strings.

DNA forms into chromosomes. Remember, the double arms are already duplicates of each other.

Chromosomes line up along centre and then the cell fibres pull them apart.

Membranes form around the two sets of chromosome threads. These become the nuclei of the two daughter cells.

The threads unwind into long strands of DNA and the whole process then starts over again.

(Note that the single chromosome threads have now duplicated themselves — see next page.)

Asexual Reproduction

ORDINARY CELL DIVISION produces new cells *identical* to the original cell. This is how all plants and animals *grow* and produce *replacement cells*. Cells throughout our body *divide* and *multiply* by this process. However some organisms also *reproduce* using ordinary cell division, *bacteria* being a good example. This is known as *asexual* reproduction. Here is a *DEFINITION* of it, for you to learn:

> In ASEXUAL REPRODUCTION there is only ONE parent, and the offspring therefore have *exactly the same genes* as the parent (i.e. they're clones — see P. 66).

This is because all the cells *in both parent and offspring* were produced by *ordinary cell division*, so they must all have *identical genes* in their cell nuclei. Asexual reproduction therefore produces no variation. Some *plants* reproduce asexually, e.g. potatoes, strawberries and daffodils (see P. 66).

Now that I have your undivided attention...

You need to *learn* the definition of *mitosis* and the sequence of diagrams, and also the definition of *asexual reproduction*. Now *cover the page* and *scribble down* the two definitions and sketch out the sequence of diagrams — *don't waste time* with neatness — just find out if you've *learnt it all* yet.

DNA Replication in Mitosis

Cell Division

Genes are Chemical Instructions

1) *A gene is a length of DNA*.
2) So DNA is a long list of *instructions* on how to put the organism together and *make it work*.
3) Each *gene* is a separate *chemical instruction* to a particular type of cell.
4) Cells make *proteins* by stringing *amino acids* together in a particular order.
5) There are only about *20 different amino acids*, but they make up *thousands* of different *proteins*.
6) Genes simply tell cells *in what order* to put the amino acids together.
7) That determines what *proteins* the cell produces, e.g. haemoglobin, or keratin, etc.
8) That in turn determines what *type of cell* it is, e.g. red blood cell, skin cell, etc.

DNA Replicates Itself to form Chromosomes

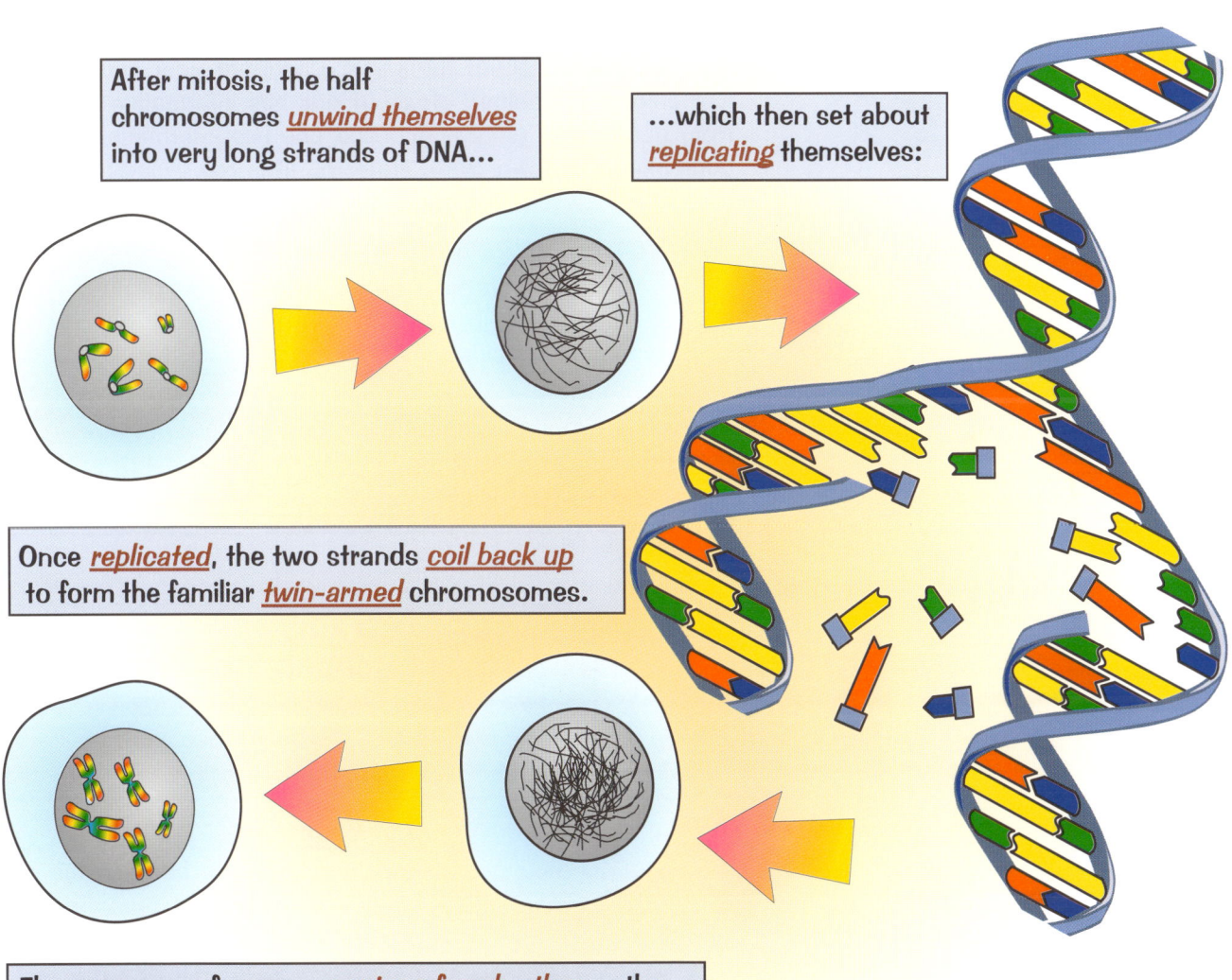

After mitosis, the half chromosomes *unwind themselves* into very long strands of DNA...

...which then set about *replicating* themselves:

Once *replicated*, the two strands *coil back up* to form the familiar *twin-armed* chromosomes.

The arms are, of course, *copies of each other* — the *two identical strands* of DNA, joined together.

Don't get all knotted up with yourself, relax and enjoy...

I have to say, I think these ace diagrams make this all very easy to learn.
You know the drill. *Cover the page* and *scribble down* all the details for both sections.

Gamete Production: Meiosis

Cell Division

You thought mitosis was exciting. Hah! You ain't seen nothing yet. <u>Meiosis</u> is the other type of cell division. It only happens in the <u>reproductive organs</u> (ovaries and testes).

> <u>MEIOSIS</u> produces <u>"cells which have half the proper number of chromosomes"</u>.
> Such cells are also known as "<u>gametes</u>".

These cells are "genetically different" from each other because <u>the genes all get shuffled up</u> during meiosis and each gamete only gets <u>half of them</u>, selected at random.
Confused? I'm not surprised. But fear not, my little yellow friend...
The diagrams below will make it a lot clearer — but you have to <u>study</u> them pretty hard.

<u>Reproductive cell</u> in testis (or ovary).

1) Remember, there are <u>23 pairs</u> of chromosomes at the start. That means 46 altogether, two of each type. In each <u>pair</u>, there is one you got from your <u>father</u>, and one you got from your <u>mother</u>.

They're called "<u>homologous pairs</u>" because <u>both</u> chromosomes have information about the <u>same aspects</u> of your body, e.g. hair colour, eye colour, etc., but one has information brought from your father (shown red) and one has information from your mother (shown blue). Note the little red y-chromosome.

2) <u>The PAIRS now split up</u> so that some of your father's chromosomes go with some of your mother's chromosomes, but there will be <u>no pairs at all now</u>. Just <u>one of each</u> of the 23 different types in each of the two new cells. Each cell therefore has a <u>mixture</u> of your mother's and father's characteristics, but only has <u>half the full complement</u> of chromosomes.

3) These cells now split <u>mitosis-style</u>, with the <u>chromosomes themselves splitting</u> to form two identical cells, called <u>gametes</u>. The twin-armed chromosomes were already duplicates, don't forget.

And that's meiosis done.
Note the difference between the <u>first stage</u> where the <u>pairs separate</u> and the <u>second stage</u> where the <u>chromosomes themselves split</u>. It's tricky!

<u>GAMETES</u>
i.e. sperm cells or (egg cells).

Meiosis? Not even remotely scary...

There's a few tricky words in there which don't help — especially if you just ignore them...
The only way to <u>learn</u> this page is by constant reference to the diagram. Make sure you can sketch all the parts of it <u>from memory</u> and <u>scribble notes</u> to explain each stage. Even so, it's still difficult to understand it all, never mind remember it. But that's what you gotta do!

NEAB Syllabus — SECTION FOUR — VARIATION, INHERITANCE & EVOLUTION

Fertilisation: Meeting of Gametes

Cell Division

There are 23 Pairs of Human Chromosomes

They are well known and numbered. In every cell nucleus we have two of each type. The diagram shows the 23 pairs of chromosomes from a human cell. One chromosome in each pair is inherited from each of our parents. Normal body cells have 46 chromosomes, in 23 homologous pairs.

Remember, "homologous" means that the two chromosomes in each pair are equivalent to each other. In other words, the number 19 chromosomes from both your parents pair off together, as do the number 17s etc. What you don't get is the number 12 chromosome from one parent pairing off with, say, the number 5 chromosome from the other.

Reproductive Cells undergo Meiosis to Produce Gametes:

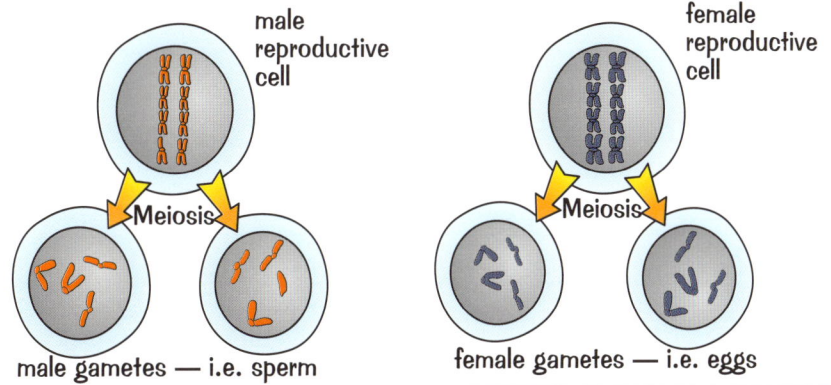

The gametes remember, only have one chromosome to describe each bit of you, one copy of each of the chromosomes numbered 1 to 23. But a normal cell needs two chromosomes of each type — one from each parent, so...

Sexual Reproduction

Fertilisation: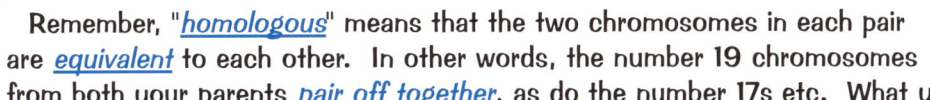

SEXUAL REPRODUCTION involves the fusion of male and female gametes (sex cells). Because there are **TWO** parents, the offspring contains _a mixture of their parents genes_.

The offspring will receive its outward characteristics as a mixture from the two sets of chromosomes, so it will inherit features from both parents. This is why sexual reproduction produces more variation than asexual reproduction. Pretty cool, eh.

WHEN THE GAMETES MEET UP during fertilisation, the 23 single chromosomes in one gamete will all pair off with their appropriate "partner chromosomes" from the other gamete to form the full 23 pairs again, No.4 with No.4, No.13 with No.13 etc. etc.

Don't forget, the two chromosomes in a pair both contain the same basic genes, e.g. for hair colour, etc. When single chromosomes meet up at fertilisation, they seek out their counterpart from the other gamete.

It should all be starting to come together now...

If you go through these last two pages you should see how the two processes, meiosis and fertilisation, are kind of opposite. Practise sketching out the sequence of diagrams, with notes, for both pages till it all sinks in. Nice, innit.

SECTION FOUR — VARIATION, INHERITANCE & EVOLUTION

Mutations

Cell Division

A MUTATION occurs when an organism develops with some *strange new characteristic* that no other member of the species has had before. For example if someone was born with blue hair it would be caused by a mutation. Some mutations are beneficial, but *most are disastrous* (e.g. blue hair).

Radiation and Certain Chemicals cause Mutations

Mutations occur 'naturally', probably caused by "natural" background radiation (from the sun, and rocks etc.) or just the laws of chance that every now and then the DNA doesn't quite copy itself properly. However *the chance of mutation is increased* by exposing yourself:

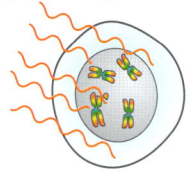

1) to *ionising radiation*, including *X-rays* and *Ultra-Violet light*, (which are the highest-frequency parts of the *EM spectrum*) together with radiation from *radioactive substances*. For each of these examples, the *greater* the *dose* of radiation, the *greater* the *chance* of mutation.

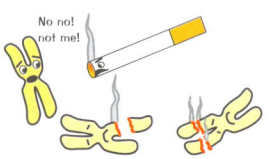

2) to certain *chemicals* which are known to cause mutations. Such chemicals are called *mutagens*. If the mutations produce cancer then the chemicals are often called *carcinogens*. Cigarette smoke contains chemical mutagens (or carcinogens).

Mutations are Caused by Faults in the DNA

There are *several ways* that mutations happen, but in the end they're all down to *faulty DNA*. Mutations *usually happen* when the DNA is *replicating itself* and something goes wrong. Because *DNA* is what *genes* are made of, and also what *chromosomes* are made of, then there are several different *definitions* of what a mutation is.
However this is the one in the syllabus and you should learn it:

> A MUTATION is a change to one or more genes.

Most Mutations are Harmful

1) If a mutation occurs in *reproductive cells*, then the young may *develop abnormally* or *die* at an early stage of their development.
2) If a mutation occurs in body cells, the mutant cells may start to *multiply* in an *uncontrolled* way and *invade* other parts of the body. This is what we know as CANCER.

Some Mutations are Beneficial, giving us "EVOLUTION"

1) *Blue budgies* appeared suddenly as a mutation amongst yellow budgies. This is a good example of a *neutral effect*. It didn't harm its chances of survival and so it flourished (and at one stage, every grandma in Britain had one).
2) *Very occasionally*, a mutation will give the organism a survival *advantage* over its relatives. This is *natural selection* and *evolution* at work. A good example is a mutation in a bacteria that makes it *resistant to antibiotics*, so the mutant gene *lives on*, in the offspring, creating a *resistant "strain"* of bacteria.

Don't get your genes in a twist, this stuff's easy...

There are four sections with numbered points for each. *Memorise* the headings and learn the numbered points, then *cover the page* and *scribble down* everything you can remember. I know it makes your head hurt, but every time you try to remember the stuff, the more it sinks in. It'll all be worth it in the end.

NEAB Syllabus — SECTION FOUR — VARIATION, INHERITANCE & EVOLUTION

X and Y Chromosomes

Genetics and DNA

There are <u>23 matched pairs</u> of chromosomes in every human body cell. You'll notice the <u>23rd</u> pair are labelled <u>XY</u>. They're the two chromosomes that <u>decide whether you turn out male or female</u>. They're called the X and Y chromosomes because they look like an X and a Y.

> **ALL MEN** have <u>an X</u> and <u>a Y</u> chromosome: **XY**
> The <u>Y chromosome is</u> **DOMINANT** and causes <u>male characteristics</u>.
>
> **ALL WOMEN** have <u>two X chromosomes</u>: **XX**
> The XX combination allows <u>female characteristics</u> to develop.

The diagram below shows the way the male XY chromosomes and female XX chromosomes <u>split up to form the gametes</u> (eggs or sperm), and then <u>combine together at fertilisation</u>.
  The criss cross lines show all the <u>possible</u> ways the X and Y chromosomes <u>could</u> combine. Remember, <u>only one of these</u> would actually happen for any offspring.
  What the diagram shows us is the <u>RELATIVE PROBABILITY</u> of each type of zygote (offspring) occurring.

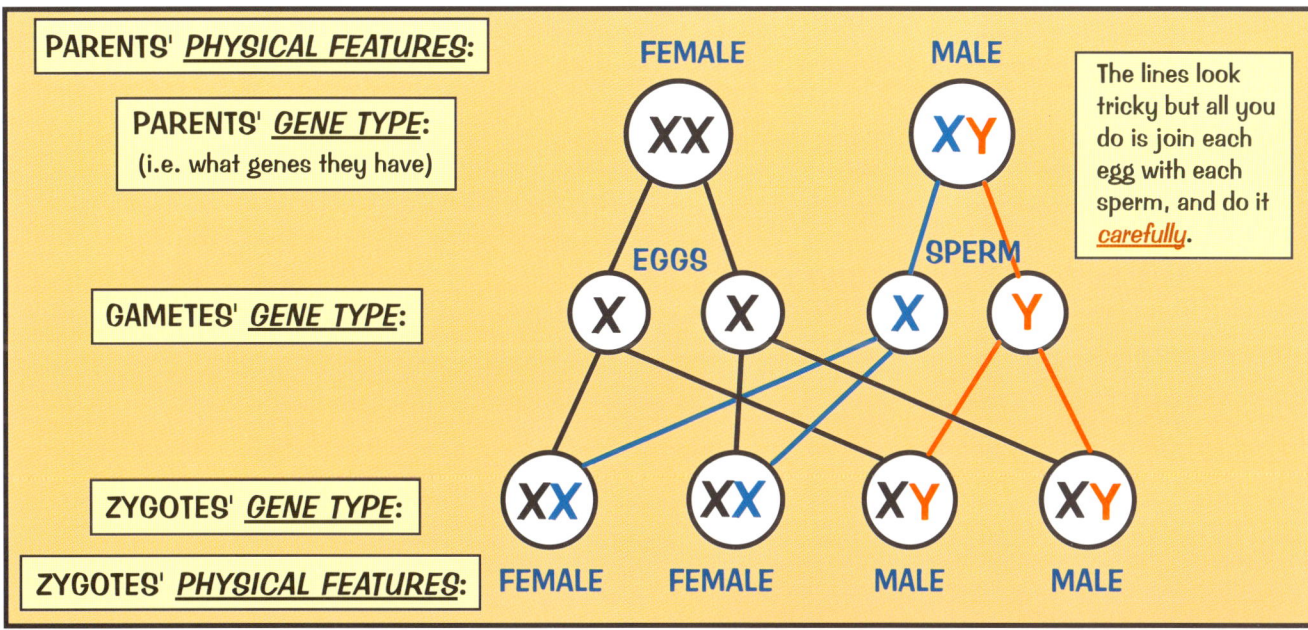

The other way of doing this is with a <u>checkerboard</u> type diagram. If you don't understand how it works, ask "Teach" to explain it. The <u>pairs of letters</u> in the middle show the <u>gene types</u> of the possible offspring.

Both diagrams show that there'll be the <u>same proportion</u> of <u>male and female offspring</u>, because there are <u>two XX results</u> and <u>two XY results</u>.

Don't forget that this <u>50:50 ratio</u> is only a <u>probability</u>. If you had four kids they <u>could</u> all be <u>boys</u> — yes I know, terrifying isn't it?

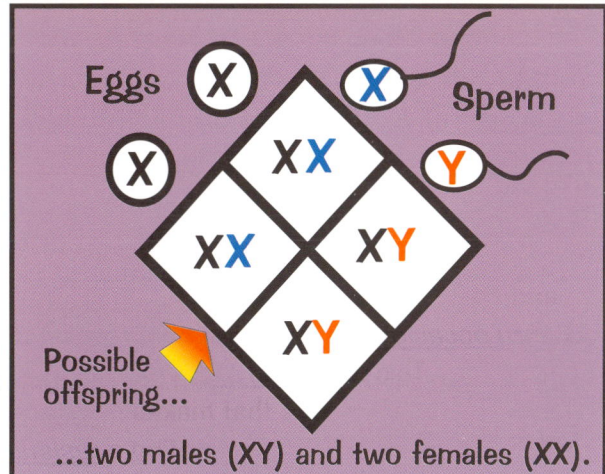

How can it take all that just to say it's a 50:50 chance...

Make sure you know all about X and Y chromosomes and who has what combination. The diagrams are real important. Practise reproducing them until you can do it <u>effortlessly</u>.

SECTION FOUR — VARIATION, INHERITANCE & EVOLUTION   NEAB SYLLABUS

Breeding Terminology

Genetics and DNA

Breeding Two Plants or Animals Who have One Gene Different

The best way to see what you get is with a diagram like either of these:

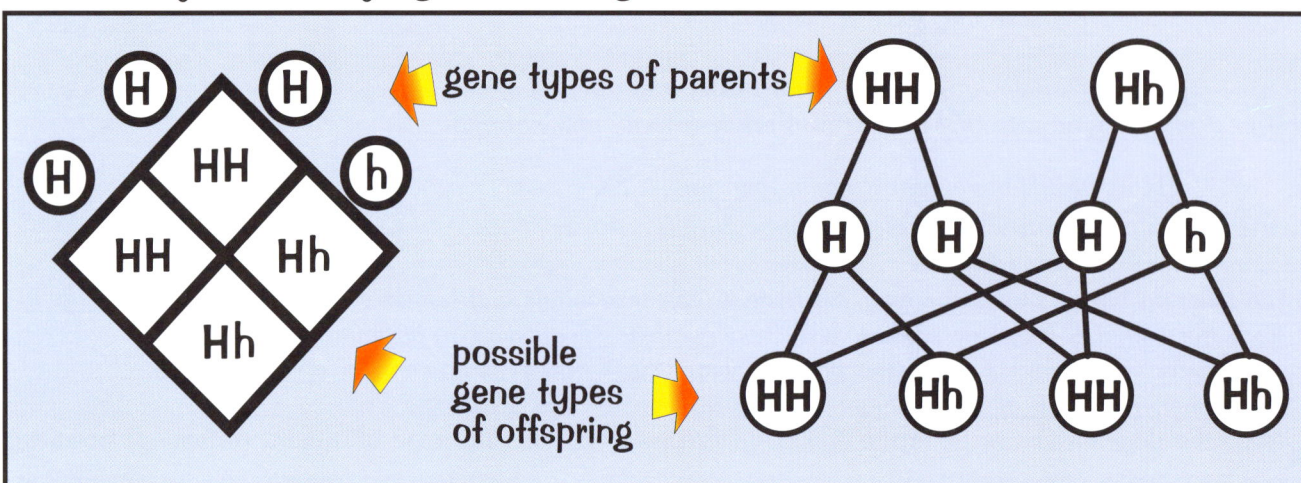

But first learn all these technical terms — it's real difficult to follow what's going on if you don't:

1) ALLELE

— this is just another name for a GENE. If you have *two different versions of a gene*, like H and h, then you have to call them ALLELES instead of genes.

2) DOMINANT AND RECESSIVE

— self explanatory. A dominant allele DOMINATES a recessive allele.

3) "PARENTAL", "F1" AND "F2" GENERATIONS

— pretty obvious. The two *originals* that you cross are the *parental generation*, their *kids* are the *F1 generation* and the "grandchildren" are the *F2 generation*. Easy peasy.

4) HOMOZYGOUS AND HETEROZYGOUS

— "Homo-" means "same kinda things", "Hetero-" means "different kinda things". They stick "-zygous" on the end to show we're talking about *genes*, (rather than any other aspect of Biology), and also just to make it *sound more complicated*, I'm certain of it. So...

"HOMOZYGOUS RECESSIVE" is the descriptive shorthand (hah!) for this: 	hh
"HOMOZYGOUS DOMINANT" is the 'shorthand' for 	HH
"HETEROZYGOUS" is the 'shorthand' for 	Hh
"A HOMOZYGOTE" or "A HETEROZYGOTE" are how you refer to people with such genes. 	

Let's try out the brilliant descriptive "shorthand" shall we:

"Alexander is homozygous recessive for the baldness gene" is *so much easier* to say and understand than *"Alex is bb"*. Hmm, well, that's Biology for you.

Now it's time to homologate your intellectual stimuli...

You can't beat a fewdal big fancyfold wordsmiths to make things crystally clearasil, can you... Anyway, half the Exam marks are for knowing the fancy words *so just keep learning 'em!*

Monohybrid Crosses: Hamsters

Genetics and DNA

Cross-breeding Hamsters

It can be all too easy to find yourself cross-breeding hamsters, some with normal hair and a mild disposition and others with wild scratty hair and a leaning towards crazy acrobatics.

Let's say that the gene which causes the crazy nature is _recessive_, so we use a _small "h"_ for it, whilst normal (boring) behaviour is due to a _dominant gene_, so we represent it with a _capital "H"_.

1) A _crazy hamster_ must have the GENE TYPE: hh.
2) However, a NORMAL HAMSTER can have TWO POSSIBLE GENE TYPES: HH or Hh.
   This is pretty important — it's the basic difference between dominant and recessive genes:

> To display RECESSIVE CHARACTERISTICS you must have
> BOTH ALLELES RECESSIVE, hh, (i.e. be "homozygous recessive")
>
> But to display DOMINANT CHARACTERISTICS you can be EITHER
> HH ("homozygous dominant") or Hh ("heterozygous").

It's only that difference which makes monohybrid crosses even _remotely_ interesting. If hh gave crazy hamsters, HH gave normal hamsters and Hh something in between, it'd all be pretty dull.

An Almost Unbearably Exciting Example

Let's take a _thoroughbred crazy hamster_, genotype hh, with a _thoroughbred normal hamster_, genotype HH, and cross breed them. You must learn this whole diagram thoroughly, till you can do it all yourself:

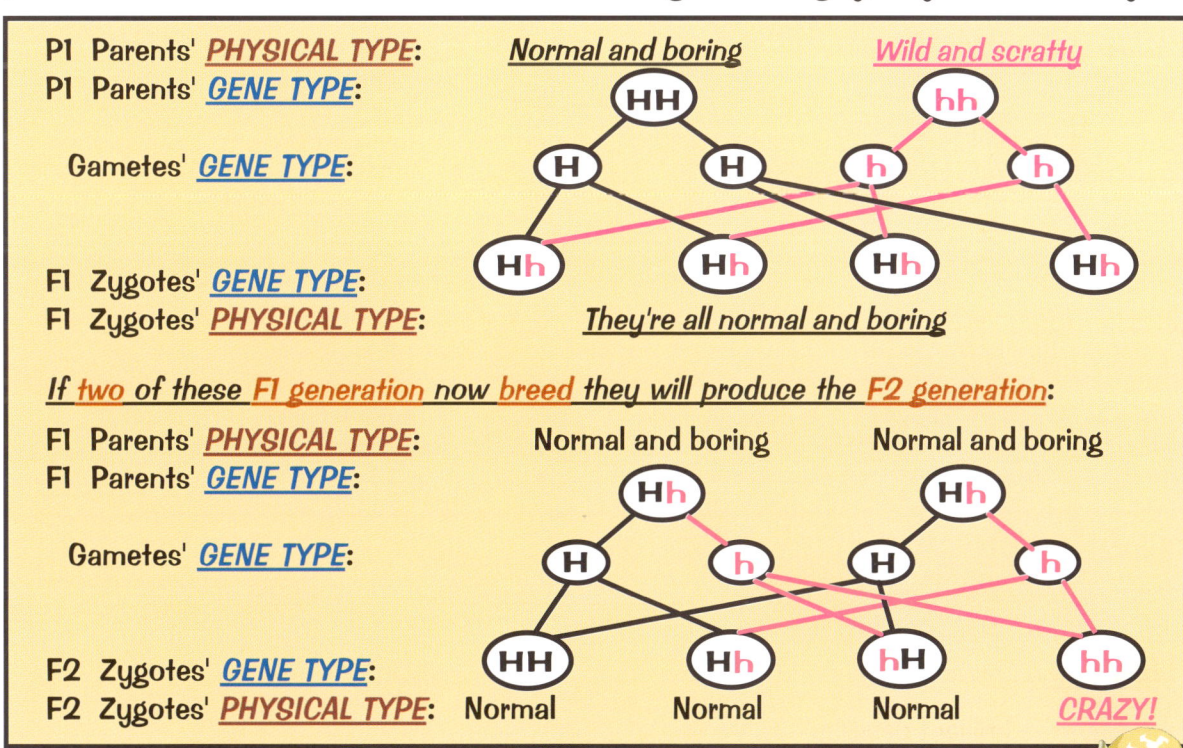

This gives a **3 : 1 RATIO** of Normal to Crazy offspring in the F2 generation.
Remember that "results" like this are only PROBABILITIES. It doesn't mean it'll happen.
(Most likely, you'll end up trying to contain a mini-riot of nine lunatic baby hamsters.)

See how those fancy words start to roll off the tongue...

The diagram and all its fancy words need to be second nature to you. So practise writing it out _from memory_ until you get it all right. Because when you can do one — _you can do 'em all_.

SECTION FOUR — VARIATION, INHERITANCE & EVOLUTION   NEAB SYLLABUS

Cystic Fibrosis

Genetics and DNA

The Symptoms

1) CYSTIC FIBROSIS is a GENETIC DISEASE which affects about 1 in 1600 people in the UK.
2) It's a disorder of the cell membranes caused by a defective gene.
3) Both parents must have the defective gene for the disorder to be passed on although both may be carriers. A carrier is somebody who has the defective gene without actually having the disorder.
4) The result of the defective gene is that the body produces a lot of thick sticky mucus in the lungs, which has to be removed by massage.
5) Excess mucus also occurs in the pancreas, causing digestive problems.
6) Much more seriously though, THE BLOCKAGE OF THE AIR PASSAGES in the lungs causes a lot of CHEST INFECTIONS. There's still no cure or effective treatment for this condition.
7) Physiotherapy and antibiotics clear them up but slowly the sufferer becomes more and more ill.

Cystic Fibrosis is Caused by a Recessive Gene (Allele)

The genetics behind cystic fibrosis is actually very straightforward.
The gene which causes cystic fibrosis is a recessive gene, c, carried by about 1 person in 20.
The usual genetic inheritance diagram illustrates what goes on:

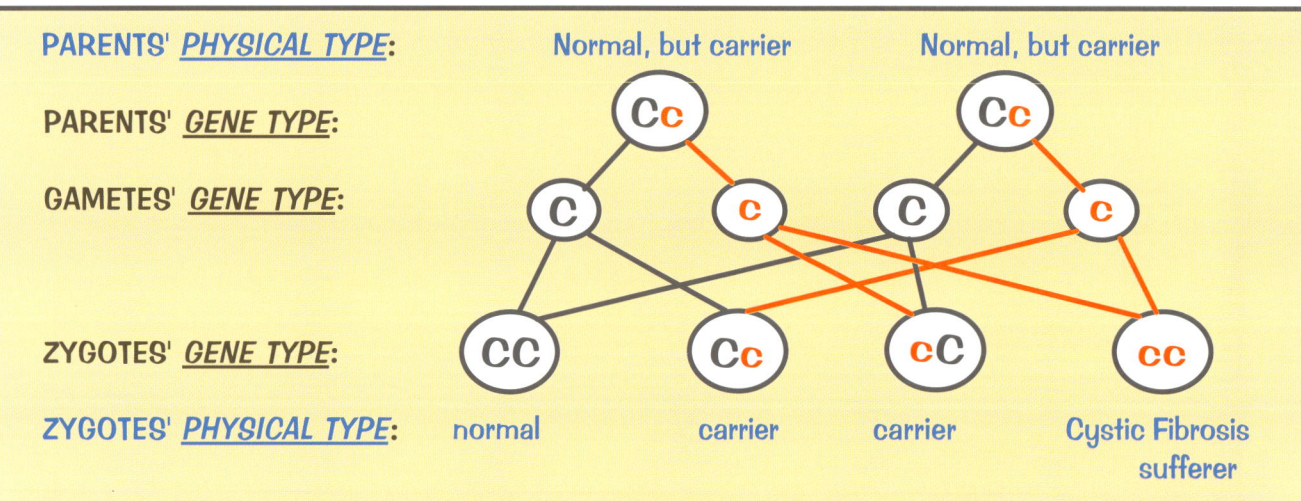

This diagram illustrates the 1 in 4 chance of a child having the disease, if both parents are carriers.

The Overall Probability is roughly 1 in 1600

1) The cystic fibrosis gene is only carried by about 1 person in 20.
   That means there's only a 1 in 400 chance that two carriers will have children together.
2) Only when BOTH PARENTS have the gene is there any chance of their children developing the disease, because the child must inherit the recessive allele, c, from BOTH parents.
3) If both parents are carriers, each baby has a 1 IN 4 CHANCE of having cystic fibrosis.
4) Remember, if one or other parent is NOT a carrier, there's no risk of any child with the disease.

It was only in 1989 that the gene causing cystic fibrosis was discovered.
Since then it has at least been possible to test parents to see if they are carriers.
Before that, the only indication was when a child suffering from the disease was actually born.
If both parents find they are carriers, there's still a difficult decision to be made about having kids.

Learn the facts then see what you know...

The symptoms and probabilities should be relatively easy to learn. The genetic diagram is also quite straightforward, once you get familiar with it. Learn the whole page, then cover it up and scribble it out.

Other Genetic Diseases

Genetics and DNA

Sickle Cell Anaemia — Caused by a Recessive Allele

1) This disease causes the RED BLOOD CELLS to be shaped like SICKLES instead of the normal round shape.
2) They then get stuck in the capillaries which deprives body cells of oxygen.
3) Parents may be carriers without actually showing the symptoms, but both parents must have the defective gene for the disease to appear in any of their children.
4) It's an unpleasant, painful disease and sufferers die at an early age.
5) Yet even though sufferers die before they can reproduce, the occurrence of sickle cell anaemia doesn't always die out as you'd expect it to, especially not in Africa.
6) This is because carriers of the recessive allele which causes it ARE MORE IMMUNE TO MALARIA. Hence, being a carrier increases their chance of survival in some parts of the world, even though some of their offspring are going to die young from sickle cell anaemia.
7) The genetics are identical to Cystic Fibrosis because both diseases are caused by a recessive allele. Hence if BOTH parents are carriers there's a 1 in 4 chance each child will develop it:

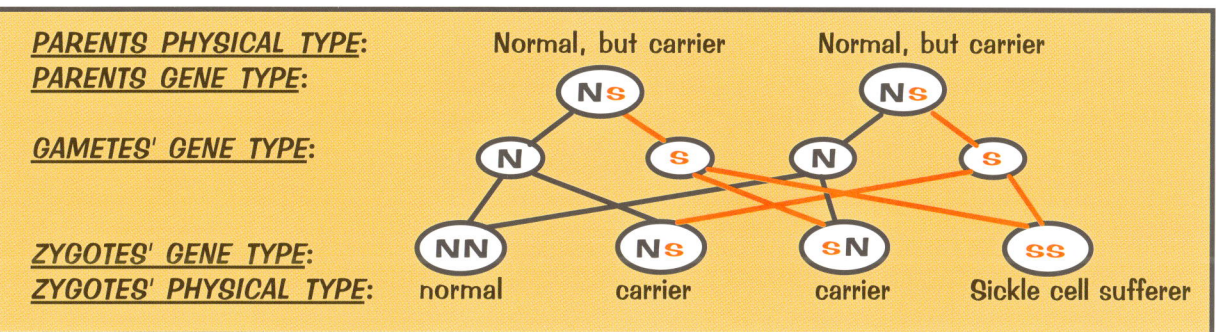

Huntington's Chorea is caused by a Dominant Allele

1) This is a disorder of the nervous system that isn't nice, resulting in shaking, erratic body movements and severe mental deterioration.
2) The disorder can be inherited from one parent who has the disorder.
3) The "carrier" parent will of course be a sufferer too since the allele is dominant, but the symptoms do not appear until after the age of 40, by which time the allele has been passed on to children and even grandchildren. Hence the disease persists.
4) UNLIKE Cystic Fibrosis and Sickle Cell Anaemia, this disease is caused by a DOMINANT allele.
5) This results in a 50% CHANCE of each child inheriting the disease IF JUST ONE PARENT is a carrier.
THESE ARE SERIOUSLY GRIM ODDS.

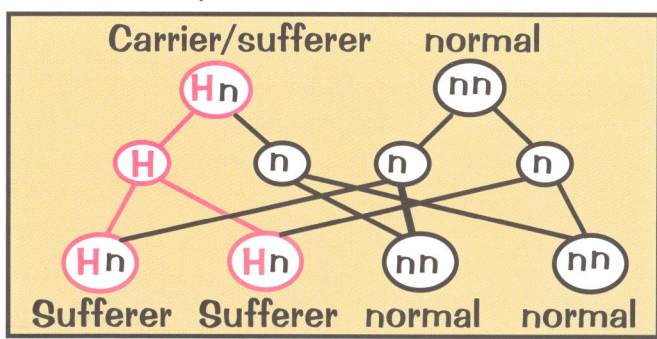

Learn the facts then see what you know...

These diseases are all mentioned in the *syllabus* and questions on them are *very likely*. You need to *learn* all this very basic information on all three. *Cover the page* and *scribble* it all down.

SECTION FOUR — VARIATION, INHERITANCE & EVOLUTION   NEAB SYLLABUS

Selective Breeding

Controlling Inheritance

Selective Breeding is Very Simple

SELECTIVE BREEDING is also called *artificial selection*, because humans artificially select the plants or animals that are going to breed and flourish, according to what WE want from them. This is the basic process involved in selective breeding:

1) From your existing stock select the ones which have the BEST CHARACTERISTICS.

2) Breed them with each other.

3) Select the best of the OFFSPRING, and combine them with the best that you already have and breed again.

4) Continue this process over SEVERAL GENERATIONS to develop the desired traits.

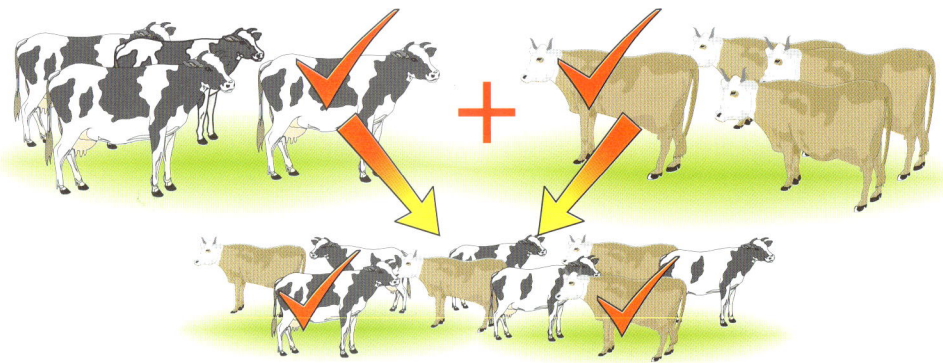

Selective Breeding is Very Useful in Farming

Artificial Selection like this is used in *most areas of modern farming*, to great benefit:

1) Better BEEF

Selectively breeding beef cattle to get the best beef (taste, texture, appearance, etc.).

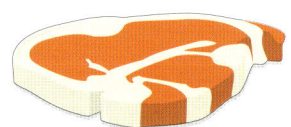

2) Better MILK

Selectively breeding milking cows to increase milk yield and resistance to disease.

3) Better CHICKENS

Selectively breeding chickens to improve egg size and number of eggs per hen.

4) Better WHEAT

Selectively breeding wheat to produce new varieties with better yields and better disease-resistance too.

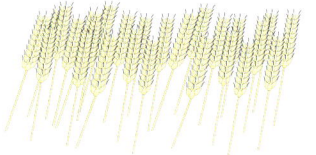

5) Better FLOWERS

Selectively breeding flowers to produce bigger and better and more colourful ones.

NEAB Syllabus — SECTION FOUR — VARIATION, INHERITANCE & EVOLUTION

Selective Breeding

Controlling Inheritance

The Main Drawback is a Reduction in the Gene Pool

In farming, animals are selectively bred to develop the best features, which are basically:

A) **MAXIMUM YIELD** of meat, milk, grain etc.

B) **GOOD HEALTH** and **DISEASE RESISTANCE**.

1) But selective breeding reduces the number of alleles in a population because the farmer keeps breeding from the "best" animals or plants — the same ones all the time.

2) This can cause serious problems if a new disease appears, as all the plants or animals could be wiped out.

3) This is made more likely because all the stock are closely related to each other, so if one of them is going to be killed by a new disease, the others are also likely to succumb to it.

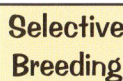 → 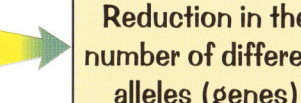 → 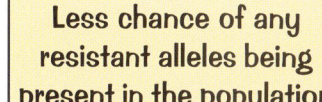 →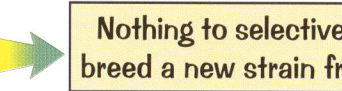

| Selective Breeding | Reduction in the number of different alleles (genes) | Less chance of any resistant alleles being present in the population | Nothing to selectively breed a new strain from |

Selective Breeding in Pedigree Dogs Causes Bad Health

Most of the above doesn't apply to selective breeding in pedigree dogs where physical appearance is the only thing that seems to matter — purely for winning dog shows. Many pedigree dogs (in fact most pedigree dogs) have quite bad health problems because of this artificial selection.

Random Cross-Breeds Can be Much Healthier Dogs

1) Mongrels (random cross-breeds) on the other hand, are usually much healthier, fitter dogs because they're not so interbred.

2) They're very often much nicer natured and they can be real pretty too.

3) The word "mongrel" does them no justice at all. If you want a really great dog, my advice is go to the dog rescue place and get a crazy cross-breed and just love him.

Don't sit there brooding over it, just learn the info...

Selective breeding is a very simple topic. In the Exam they'll likely give you half a page explaining how a farmer in Sussex did this or that with his crops or cows, and then they'll suddenly ask: "What is meant by selective breeding". That's when you just write down the four points at the top of page 64. Then they'll ask you to "Suggest other ways that selective breeding might be used by farmers in Sussex to improve their yield". That's when you just list some of the examples that you've learnt. They do like padding the questions out, don't they! In Olden Times (the 1970s) they would just have said: "Explain what selective breeding is and give four examples of where it is used. — 8 Marks" (!)

SECTION FOUR — VARIATION, INHERITANCE & EVOLUTION   NEAB SYLLABUS

Cloning

Controlling Inheritance

Learn this *definition* of clones:

CLONES are GENETICALLY IDENTICAL ORGANISMS

Clones occur *naturally* in both plants and animals. *Identical twins* are clones of each other. These days clones are very much a part of the *high-tech farming industry*.

Embryo Transplants in Cows

Normally, farmers only breed from their **BEST** cows and bulls. However, such traditional methods would only allow the *prize cow* to produce *one new offspring each year*. These days the whole process has been transformed using **EMBRYO TRANSPLANTS**:

1) **SPERM** are taken from the prize bull.
2) They're checked for *genetic defects* and which **SEX** they are.
3) They can also be **FROZEN** and used at a later date.
4) Selected prize cows are given **HORMONES** to make them produce **LOTS OF EGGS**.
5) The cows are then **ARTIFICIALLY INSEMINATED**.
6) **THE EMBRYOS** are taken from the prize cows and checked for sex and genetic defects.
7) The embryos are developed and **SPLIT** (to form **CLONES**) before any cells become specialised.
8) These embryos are **IMPLANTED** into other cows, where they grow. They can also be **FROZEN** and used at a later date.

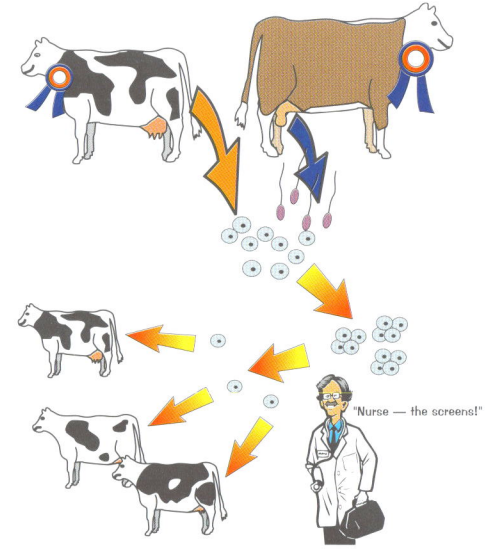
"Nurse — the screens!"

ADVANTAGES OF EMBRYO TRANSPLANTS — Hundreds of Ideal Offspring

a) *Hundreds* of "ideal" offspring can be produced *every year* from the best bull and cow.
b) The original prize cow can keep producing *prize eggs all year round*.

DISADVANTAGES — Reduced Gene Pool

Only the *usual drawback with clones* — a reduced *"gene pool"* leading to *vulnerability to new diseases*.

Many Plants Produce Clones — all by themselves

This means they produce *exact genetic copies* of themselves *without involving another plant*. Here are three common ones:

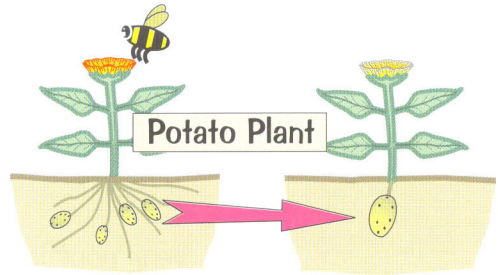

1) **STRAWBERRY PLANTS** producing *runners*.

2) New **POTATO PLANTS** growing from tubers of old plant.

3) *Bulbs* such as **DAFFODILS** growing new bulbs off the side of them.

NEAB Syllabus — Section Four — Variation, Inheritance & Evolution

Cloned Plants

Controlling Inheritance

Making Clones from Cuttings

1) Gardeners are familiar with taking *cuttings* from good parent plants, and then planting them to produce *identical copies* (clones) of the parent plant.
2) The cuttings are kept in a *damp atmosphere* until their *roots develop*.
3) These plants can be produced *quickly and cheaply*.

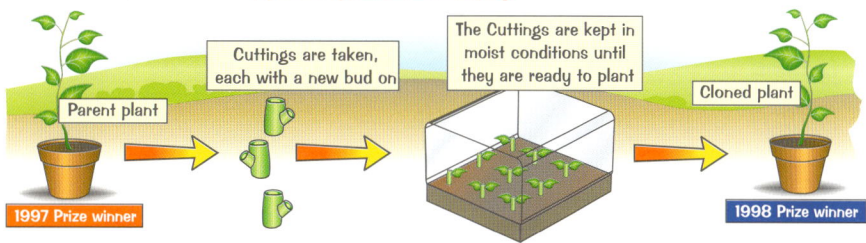

4) These days, this basic technique has been given the *full high-tech treatment* by *commercial plant breeders*:

The Essentials of Commercial Cloning:

TISSUE CULTURE

This is where, instead of starting with at least a stem and bud, they just put *A FEW PLANT CELLS* in a *growth medium* with *hormones* and it just grows into *A NEW PLANT*. Just like that! Phew.

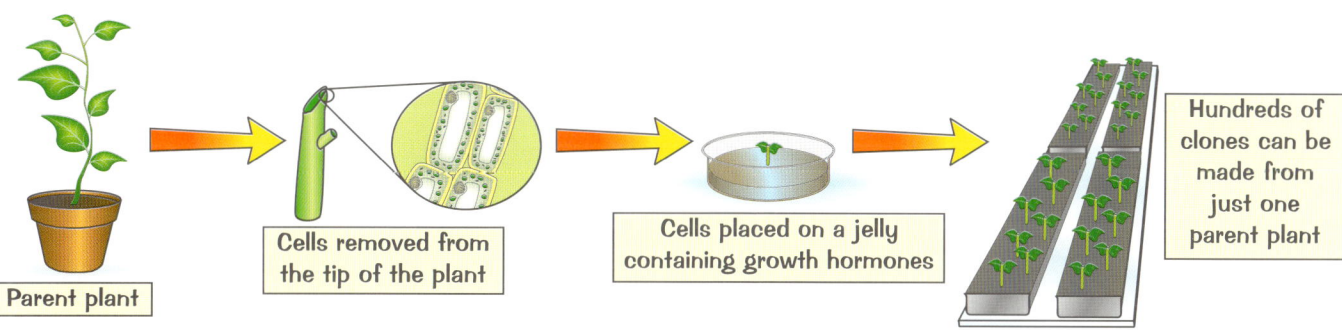

ADVANTAGES OF TISSUE CULTURE:

1) Very *FAST* — can produce thousands of plantlets in a few weeks.
2) Very little *SPACE* needed.
3) *CAN GROW ALL YEAR* — no problem with weather or seasons.
4) New plants are *DISEASE-FREE*.
5) *NEW PLANTS* can be *DEVELOPED* (very quickly) by splicing new genes into plantlets and seeing how they turn out.

DISADVANTAGES OF TISSUE CULTURE:

Only the usual drawback with clones — *a reduced "gene pool"* leading to *vulnerability to new diseases*.

Stop Cloning Around and just learn it...

I hope you realise that they could easily test your knowledge of *any* sentence on this page. I only put in stuff you need to know, you know. Practise scribbling out all the facts on this page, *mini-essay style*.

SECTION FOUR — VARIATION, INHERITANCE & EVOLUTION

Genetic Engineering

Controlling Inheritance

Genetic Engineering is Ace — hopefully

This is a new science with exciting possibilities, but *dangers* too. The basic idea is to move sections of <u>DNA</u> (genes) from one organism to another so that it produces <u>useful biological products</u>. We presently use bacteria to produce <u>human insulin</u> for diabetes sufferers and also to produce <u>human growth hormone</u> for children who aren't growing properly.

Genetic Engineering involves these Important Stages:

1) The useful gene is "<u>CUT</u>" from the DNA of say a human.
2) This is done using <u>ENZYMES</u>.
   Particular enzymes will cut out particular bits of DNA.
3) <u>ENZYMES</u> are then used to <u>cut the DNA</u> of a <u>bacterium</u> and the human gene is then inserted.
4) Again this "<u>SPLICING</u>" of a new gene is controlled by certain <u>specific enzymes</u>.
5) The bacterium is now <u>CULTIVATED</u> and soon there are <u>millions</u> of similar bacteria all producing, say human insulin.
6) This can be done on an <u>INDUSTRIAL SCALE</u> and the useful product can be <u>separated out</u>.

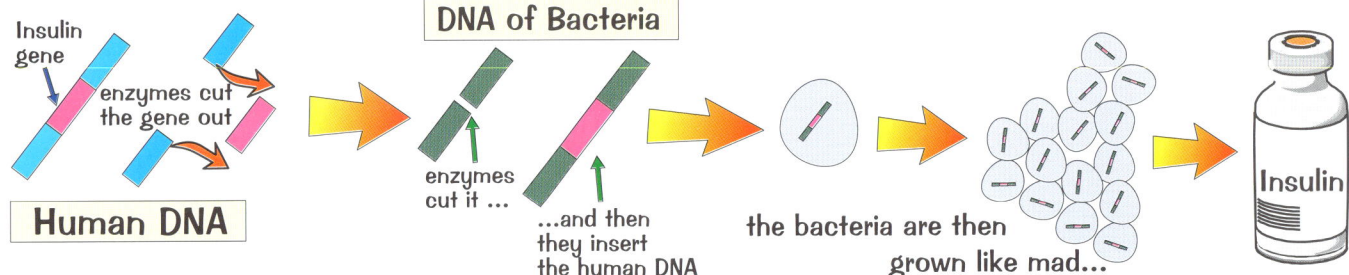

Hence we've turned nasty old bacteria into <u>a useful biological factory</u>.
Phew, that's modern science for you.

Using Animals as Chemists

1) The same approach can also be used to <u>transfer useful genes into ANIMAL EMBRYOS</u>. Sheep for example can be developed which produce useful substances (i.e. drugs) in <u>their milk!</u> This is a very easy way to produce drugs...

2) Insects also have their uses. <u>Mosquitos</u> may, in the near future, be used to combat diseases such as "<u>malaria</u>". The mosquitos that normally spread malaria are being <u>genetically engineered</u> to produce the malaria vaccine. Therefore instead of giving the disease to people they will soon hopefully be <u>immunising</u> them instead.

Nothing's been done to stop the itching though.

Hmmph... Kids these days, they're all the same...

Once again, they could ask you about any of the details on this page. The only way to be sure you know it: <u>cover the page</u> and write <u>mini-essays</u> on both topics. Then see what you missed, and <u>try again</u>...

NEAB Syllabus — SECTION FOUR — VARIATION, INHERITANCE & EVOLUTION

Evolution

The Theory of Evolution is Cool

1) This suggests that all the animals and plants on Earth gradually "evolved" over millions of years, rather than just suddenly popping into existence. Makes sense.

2) Life on Earth began as simple organisms living in water and gradually everything else evolved from there. And it only took about 3,000,000,000 years.

Fossils Provide Evidence for it

1) Fossils provide lots of evidence for evolution.
2) They show how today's species have changed and developed over millions of years.
3) There are quite a few "missing links" though because the fossil record is incomplete.
4) This is because very very few dead plants or animals actually turn into fossils.
5) Most just decay away completely.

The Evolution of The Horse is Ace

1) One set of fossils which *is* pretty good though is that showing the evolution of the horse.
2) This developed from quite a small creature about the size of a dog and the fossils show how the middle toe slowly became bigger and bigger and eventually evolved into the familiar hoof of today's horse.
3) It took about 60 million years though.
4) This is pretty strong evidence in support of evolution because it really shows evolution happening!

Forefeet — **Evolution of the horse**

Hyracotherium

Mesohippus

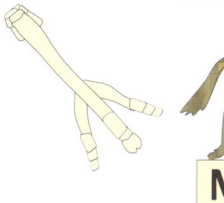 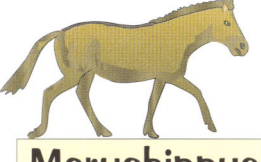
Merychippus

Pliohippus

Modern

Extinction is Pretty Bad News

The dinosaurs and hairy mammoths became EXTINCT and it's only FOSSILS that tell us they ever existed at all, (notwithstanding the odd questionable glacier story).

There are THREE WAYS a species can become EXTINCT:
1) The ENVIRONMENT CHANGES too quickly.
2) A new PREDATOR or DISEASE kills them all.
3) They can't COMPETE with another (new) species for FOOD.

As the environment slowly changes, it will gradually favour certain new characteristics amongst the members of the species and over many generations those features will proliferate. In this way, the species constantly adapts to its changing environment. But if the environment changes too fast the whole species may be wiped out, i.e. extinction...

Stop horsing around and just learn the facts...

Another stupefyingly easy page to learn. Use the mini-essay method. Just make sure you learn every fact, that's all. Dinosaurs never did proper revision and look what happened to them. (Mind you they did last about 200 million years, which is about 199.9 million more than we have, so far...)

Fossils

Evolution

FOSSILS are the "remains" of plants and animals which lived millions of years ago.

There are Three ways that Fossils can be Formed:

1) From the hard parts of animals.
2) From the softer parts of plants or animals.
3) When no decay happens at all.

1) Fossils Usually Form from the Hard Parts of animals:

1) It's usually the hardest parts of animals like bones, teeth, shells, etc., which eventually become fossils.

2) That's because these things don't don't decay easily, so they tend to last a long time when buried.

3) Eventually they are replaced by minerals as they decay, forming a rock-like substance shaped like the original hard part.

4) The surrounding sediment also turns to rock, but the fossil stays distinct inside until eventually someone digs it up.

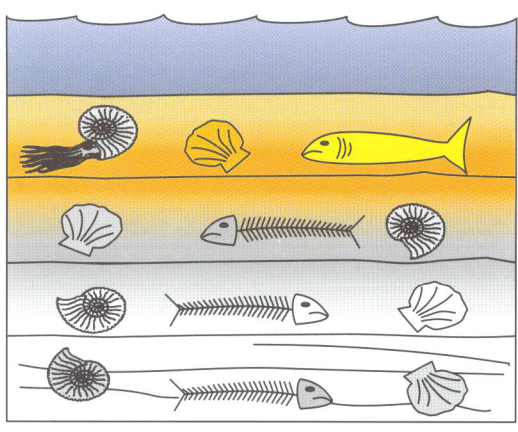

2) Fossils Can Form from Softer Parts of animals:

1) Sometimes fossils are formed from the softer parts which somehow haven't decayed.

2) The soft material gradually becomes "petrified" (turns to stone) as it slowly decays and is replaced by minerals.

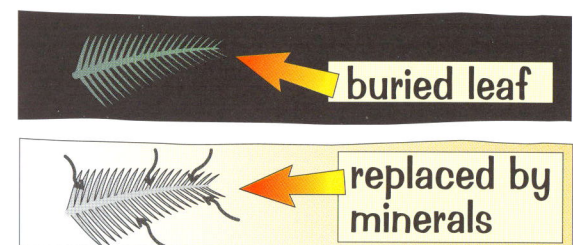

3) This is rare, since there are very few occasions when decay occurs so slowly.

4) Most plant fossils are of this type because plants are generally soft and decay quickly.

5) For petrification to happen, the plant or animal usually has to fall into a swamp or bog and be covered quickly.

6) If there is virtually no oxygen reaching the plant it will not decay quickly, and petrification can gradually take place.

Fossils

Evolution

3) *In Places Where No Decay Happens:*

Where no decay whatsoever happens, then the _whole original plant or animal_ may survive for _thousands of years_. There are THREE IMPORTANT EXAMPLES:

a) **AMBER** — no **OXYGEN** or **MOISTURE** for the _decay microbes_.

INSECTS are often found _fully preserved_ in amber, which is a clear yellow "stone" made of **FOSSILISED RESIN** that ran out of an ancient tree hundreds of millions of years ago, engulfing the insect.

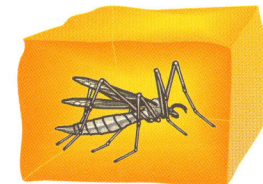

b) **GLACIERS** — too **COLD** for the _decay microbes_ to work.

A **HAIRY MAMMOTH** was found fully preserved in a glacier somewhere several years ago.

(at least that's what I heard, though I never saw any pictures of it so maybe it was a hoax, I'm not really sure, but anyway in principle one could turn up any time...)

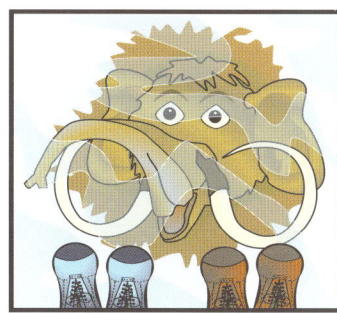

c) **WATERLOGGED BOGS** — too **ACIDIC** for _decay microbes_.

A _10,000 year old man_ was found in a bog a few years ago. He was dead, and a bit squashed but otherwise quite well preserved, although it was clear he had been _murdered_.

(Police are not looking for witnesses and have asked anyone *else* who thinks they may have important information to just keep away.)

Evidence from Rock and Soil Strata

The fossils found in _rock layers_ tell us TWO THINGS:

1) What the creatures and plants **LOOKED LIKE**.

2) **HOW LONG AGO THEY EXISTED**, by the type of rock they're in.

Generally speaking, the **DEEPER** you find the fossil, the **OLDER** it will be, though of course rocks get pushed upwards and eroded, so very old rocks can become exposed.

Fossils are usually _dated_ by geologists who **ALREADY KNOW THE AGE OF THE ROCK**. The Grand Canyon in Arizona is about _1 mile deep_. It was formed by a river slowly cutting down through layers of rock. The rocks at the bottom are about _1,000,000,000 years old_, and the fossil record in the sides is pretty cool.

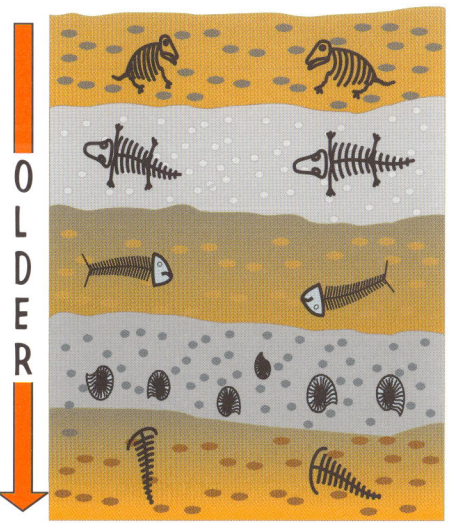

Don't get bogged down in all this information...

Make sure you're fully aware of the _three_ different types of _fossil_ and how they're _formed_. Also make sure you learn all the details about what information rocks provide. Many people read stuff and then think they know it. It's only if you _cover it up_ that you find out what you _really_ know.

Natural Selection

Evolution

Darwin's Theory of Natural Selection is Ace

1) THIS THEORY IS COOL and provides a comprehensive explanation for all life on Earth.

2) Mind you, it caused some trouble at the time, because for the first time ever, there was a highly plausible explanation for our own existence, without the need for a "Creator".

3) This was bad news for the religious authorities of the time, who tried to ridicule old Charlie's ideas. But, as they say, "THE TRUTH WILL OUT".

Darwin made Four Important Observations...

1) All organisms produce MORE OFFSPRING than could possibly survive.

2) But in fact, population numbers tend to remain FAIRLY CONSTANT over long periods of time.

3) Organisms in a species show WIDE VARIATION due to different genes.

4) SOME of the variations are INHERITED AND PASSED ON to the next generation.

...and then made these Two Deductions:

1) Since most offspring don't survive, all organisms must have to STRUGGLE FOR SURVIVAL. (Predation, disease and competition cause large numbers of individuals to die).

2) The ones who SURVIVE AND REPRODUCE will PASS ON THEIR GENES.

This is the famous "SURVIVAL OF THE FITTEST" statement. Organisms with slightly less survival-value will probably perish first, leaving the strongest and fittest to pass on their genes to the next generation.

Mutations play a big part in Natural Selection...

...by creating a new feature with a high survival value. Once upon a time maybe all rabbits had short ears and managed OK. Then one day out popped a mutant with BIG EARS who was always the first to dive for cover. Pretty soon he's got a whole family of them with BIG EARS, all diving for cover before the other rabbits, and before you know it there's only BIG-EARED rabbits left because the rest just didn't hear trouble coming quick enough. *(Eat your heart out, Rudyard Kipling)*

FOX!

NEAB Syllabus *Section Four — Variation, Inheritance & Evolution*

Natural Selection

Evolution

A Modern Example — Flat Cockroaches

A recent creepy crawly example of _evolution_ through _natural selection_ is all too apparent in many kitchens around the world.

1) As health inspectors wage war on them, little do they realise how much the _cockroach_ has gone out of its way to fit in.

2) Over the centuries, as man and cockroaches have _shared accommodation_ the cockroaches have actually become _smaller and flatter_ to adapt to our domestic environment.

3) In each generation the smaller, flatter offspring find _easier access_ to our larders and _more places to hide_, while the _larger, bulkier_ offspring get squashed out.

All Wild Creatures live in a very Harsh World indeed...

The _natural world_ may seem like a paradise on Earth to a lot of people, but the _reality_ for the wild creatures that live in it is quite different.

The natural world is in fact a very harsh environment where many offspring DIE YOUNG, due to PREDATORS, DISEASE and COMPETITION.

But remember, _this is an important element_ in the process of NATURAL SELECTION. There has to be _a LARGE SURPLUS of offspring_ for nature to _select the fittest_ from.

Farms are Much Easier...

Life for any _farm animal_ is a veritable dream compared to the "_eat or be eaten_" savage reality of the 'natural' world.

Most wild animals are eventually either _eaten alive_ or else they _starve to death_. Think about it — _they've all gotta go somehow_. Give them a nice cosy civilised farm any day, I say...

"Natural Selection" — sounds like Vegan Chocolates...

These two pages are split into five sections. _Memorise_ the headings, then _cover the page_ and _scribble down_ all you can about each section. Keep trying until you can _remember_ all the important points.

SECTION FOUR — VARIATION, INHERITANCE & EVOLUTION

NEAB SYLLABUS

Revision Summary for Section Four

Gee, all that business about genes and chromosomes and the like — it's all pretty serious stuff, don't you think? It takes a real effort to get your head round it all. There's too many big fancy words, for one thing. But there you go — life's tough and you've just gotta face up to it.
Use these questions to find out what you know — and what you don't. Then look back and learn the bits you didn't know. Then try the questions again, and again...

1) What are the two types of variation? Describe their relative importance for plants and animals.
2) List four features of animals which aren't affected at all by environment, and four which are.
3) On P. 52 there are 12 fancy words to do with genetics. List them all — with explanations.
4) Draw a set of diagrams showing the relationship between: cell, nucleus, chromosomes, genes, DNA.
5) Give a definition of mitosis. Draw a set of diagrams showing what happens in mitosis.
6) What is asexual reproduction? Give a proper definition for it. How does it involve mitosis?
7) Genes are chemical instructions. Give details of exactly what instructions they give.
8) Where does meiosis take place? What kind of cells does meiosis produce?
9) Draw out the sequence of diagrams showing what happens during meiosis.
10) How many pairs of chromosomes are there in a normal human cell nucleus?
11) What happens to the chromosome numbers during meiosis and then during fertilisation?
12) Give an example of harmful, neutral and beneficial mutations.
13) Name three things that increase the chance of a mutation occurring.
14) What are X and Y chromosomes to do with? Who has what combination?
15) Copy and complete the genetic inheritance diagram and the checker-board diagram to show how these genes are passed on.

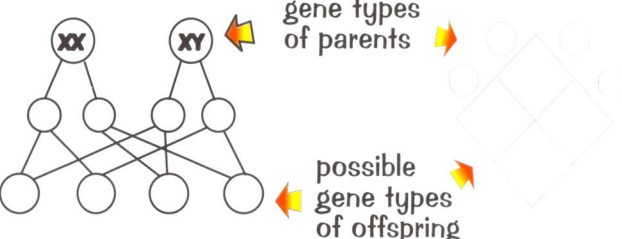

16) Give brief explanations of the following words:
    a) Allele; b) Homozygous; c) Heterozygous.
17) What are the fancy terms given to the following combinations of genes:
    a) HH; b) hh; c) Hh.
18) Starting with parental gene types HH and hh, draw a full genetic inheritance diagram to show the eventual gene types and physical types of the F1 and F2 generations (of hamsters).
19) List the symptoms and treatment of cystic fibrosis. What causes this disease?
20) Draw a genetics diagram to show the probability of a child being a sufferer (assume each parent is a carrier).
21) What is the chance of a child not being a carrier or a sufferer?
22) Give the cause and symptoms of sickle cell anaemia. Why does it not die out?
23) Explain the grim odds for Huntington's Chorea.
24) Describe the basic procedure in selective breeding (of cows). Give five other examples.
25) What is the main drawback of selective breeding in   a) farming   b) pedigree dogs?
26) Write down all you know on cloned plants.
27) Give a good account of embryo transplants, and a good account of genetic engineering.
28) Describe the drawbacks and ethical problems concerning the use of genetic engineering.
29) Describe fully the three ways that fossils can form. Give examples of each type.
30) Explain how fossils found in rocks support the theory of evolution. Refer to the horse.
31) What were Darwin's four observations and two deductions?
32) Describe two examples of how natural selection changes animals. Is it a cosy life for wild animals?

LIVING THINGS IN THEIR ENVIRONMENT

Population Size & Distribution

Adaptation and Competition

Four Factors affect the Individual Organisms

These four physical factors fluctuate throughout the day and year. Organisms *live, grow* and *reproduce* in places where, and at times when, these conditions are suitable.

1) The TEMPERATURE — this is rarely ideal for any organism.
2) The availability of WATER — vital to all living organisms.
3) The AMOUNT OF LIGHT AVAILABLE — this is most important to plants, but it also affects the visibility for animals.
4) OXYGEN and CARBON DIOXIDE — these affect respiration and photosynthesis respectively.

The Size of any Population depends on Five Factors

1) The TOTAL AMOUNT OF FOOD or nutrients available.
2) The amount of COMPETITION there is (from other species) for the same food or nutrients.
3) The AMOUNT OF LIGHT AVAILABLE (this applies only to plants really).
4) The NUMBER OF PREDATORS (or grazers) who may eat the animal (or plant) in question.
5) DISEASE.

All these factors help to explain why the *types* of organisms vary from *place to place* and from *time to time*.

The dynamics of plant and animal populations are really quite similar:
Plants often compete with each other for *space*, and for *water* and *nutrients* from the soil.
Animals often compete with each other for *space*, *food* and *water*.

Generally organisms will thrive best if:

1) THERE'S PLENTY OF THE GOOD THINGS IN LIFE: food, water, space, shelter, light, etc.
2) THEY'RE BETTER THAN THE COMPETITION AT GETTING IT (better *adapted*).
3) THEY DON'T GET EATEN.
4) THEY DON'T GET ILL.

That's pretty much the long and the short of it, wouldn't you say? So learn those four things. Every species is different, of course, but those FOUR basic principles will always apply.

In Exam questions YOU have to apply them to any new situation to work out what'll happen.

Revision stress — don't let it eat you up...

It's a strange topic is population sizes. In a way it seems like common sense, but it all seems to get so messy. Anyway, *learn all the points on this page* and you'll be OK with it, I'd think.

Adapt and Survive

Adaptation and Competition

If you _learn the features_ that make these animals and plants well adapted, you'll be able to apply them to any other similar creatures they might give you in the Exam.
Chances are you'll get a _camel_, _cactus_ or _polar bear_ anyway.

The Polar Bear — Designed for Arctic Conditions

The _Polar bear_ has all these features: (which _many other arctic creatures_ have too, so think on...)

1) _Large size_ and _compact shape_ (i.e. rounded), including dinky little ears, to keep the _surface area_ to a _minimum_ (compared to the body weight) — this all _reduces heat loss_.

2) A thick layer of _blubber_ for _insulation_ and also to survive hard times when food is scarce.

3) _Thick hairy coat_ for keeping the body heat in.

4) _Greasy fur_ which _sheds water_ after swimming to _prevent cooling_ due to evaporation.

5) _White fur_ to match the surroundings for _camouflage_.

6) _Strong swimmer_ to catch food in the water and _strong runner_ to run down prey on land.

7) _Big feet_ to _spread the weight_ on snow and ice.

The Camel — Designed for Desert Conditions

The _camel_ has all these features: (most of which are shared by _other desert creatures_...)

1) It can _store_ a lot of _water_ without problem. It can drink up to _20 gallons_ at once.

2) It _loses very little water_. There's little _urine_ and very little _sweating_.

3) It can tolerate _big changes_ in its own _body temperature_ to remove the need for sweating.

4) _Large feet_ to _spread load_ on soft sand.

5) All _fat_ is stored in the _hump_, there is _no layer of body fat_. This helps it to _lose_ body heat.

6) _Large surface area_. The shape of a camel is anything but compact, which gives it more surface area to _lose body heat_ to its surroundings.

7) Its _sandy colour_ gives good _camouflage_.

The Cactus is also Well Adapted for the Desert

1) It has _no leaves_ — to _reduce water loss_.

2) It has a _small surface area_ compared to its size which also _reduces water loss_. *(1000 x less than normal plants)*

3) It _stores water_ in its thick stem.

4) _Spines_ stop herbivores _eating_ them.

5) _Shallow_ but very extensive roots ensure water is _absorbed_ quickly over a large area.

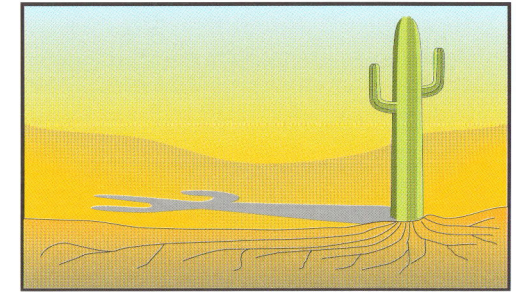

NEAB Syllabus   SECTION FIVE — LIVING THINGS IN THEIR ENVIRONMENT

Predators and Prey

Adaptation and Competition

The Lion — a perfect Predator

1) *Strong*, *agile* and *fast*.
2) *Strong jaws* and *sharp teeth* for killing prey.
3) Good *stereo vision* with both eyes *facing forwards*.
4) *Camouflaged body* for stalking prey.
5) The right sort of *teeth* for *chewing meat*.

The Rabbit — a perfect Prey

1) *Fast* and *agile* for escaping capture.
2) Eyes on sides for *all-round vision*.
3) *Big ears* for good hearing.
4) *Brown colour* for *camouflage*.
5) *White tail* to alert pals.

Populations of Prey and Predators go in Cycles

In a community containing prey and predators (as most of them do of course):

1) The <u>POPULATION</u> of any species is usually *limited* by the amount of *FOOD* available.
2) If the population of the <u>PREY</u> increases, then so will the population of the <u>PREDATORS</u>.
3) However as the population of predators <u>INCREASES</u>, the number of prey will <u>DECREASE</u>.

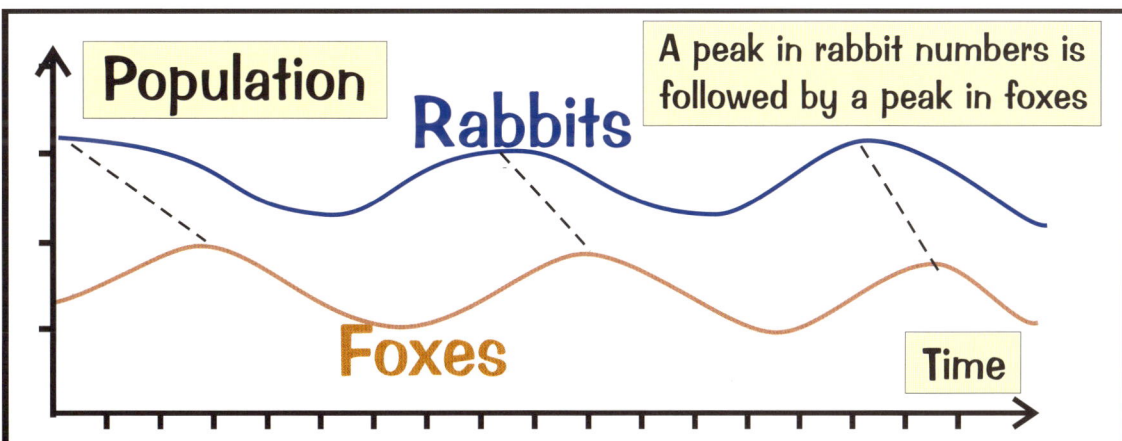

A peak in rabbit numbers is followed by a peak in foxes

i.e. *More grass* means *more rabbits*. More rabbits means *more foxes*. But more foxes means fewer *rabbits*. Eventually fewer rabbits will mean *fewer foxes again*. This *up and down pattern* continues...

Creature features — learn and survive...

It's worth learning all these survival features well enough to be able to write them down *from memory*. There's a whole world full of animals and plants, all with different survival features, but explaining them eventually becomes kinda "common sense", because the same principles tend to apply to them all.

SECTION FIVE — LIVING THINGS IN THEIR ENVIRONMENT   NEAB SYLLABUS

There's Too Many People

Human Impact on the Environment

There's one born every minute — and it's too many

1) The <u>population of the world</u> is currently <u>rising out of control</u> as the graph shows.
2) This is mostly due to <u>modern medicine</u> which has stopped widespread death from <u>disease</u>.
3) It's also due to <u>modern farming methods</u> which can now provide the <u>food</u> needed for so many hungry mouths.
4) The <u>death rate</u> is now <u>much lower</u> than the <u>birth rate</u> in many under-developed countries.
   In other words there are <u>lots more babies born</u> than people <u>dying</u>.
5) This creates <u>big problems</u> for those countries trying to cope with all those extra people.
6) Even providing <u>basic health care</u> and <u>education</u> (about contraception!) is difficult, never mind finding them <u>places to live</u>, and <u>food to eat</u>.

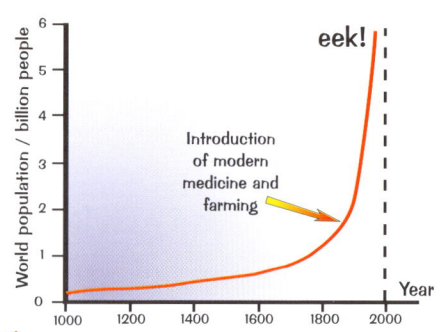

Increasing living Standards Adds Even More Pressure

The rapidly increasing population is not the only pressure on the environment. The <u>increasing standard of living</u> amongst more <u>developed countries</u> also demands more from the environment. These <u>two</u> factors mean that:

1) Raw materials, including <u>non-renewable energy resources</u>, are rapidly being used up;
2) <u>more and more waste</u> is being produced;
3) unless waste is properly handled <u>more pollution</u> will be caused.

When the Earth's population was much smaller, the effects of human activity were usually small and local.

More People Means Less Land for Plants and Animals

There are <u>four</u> main ways that humans <u>reduce</u> the amount of land available for other <u>animals</u> and <u>plants</u>.

1) <u>Building</u>

2) <u>Farming</u>

3) <u>Dumping Waste</u>

4) <u>Quarrying</u>

More People Means More Environmental Damage

Human activity can pollute all three parts of the environment:
1) <u>Water</u> – with sewage, fertiliser and toxic chemicals;
2) <u>Air</u> – with smoke and gases such as sulphur dioxide;
3) <u>Land</u> – with toxic chemicals, such as pesticides and herbicides. These may then be washed from the land into water.

Learn the facts first — then you can build your rocket...

It's real scary innit — the way that graph of world population seems to be pointing nearly vertically upwards... tricky. Anyway, you just worry about your Exams instead, and make sure you learn all the grim facts. Four sections — <u>mini-essays</u> for each, <u>till you know it all</u>.

NEAB SYLLABUS   *SECTION FIVE — LIVING THINGS IN THEIR ENVIRONMENT*

Acid Rain

Human Impact on the Environment

Burning Fossil Fuels Causes Acid Rain

1) When _fossil fuels_ are _burned_ they release mostly _carbon dioxide_ which is causing the _Greenhouse Effect_ (see P. 81). They also release _two_ other _harmful gases_: a) SULPHUR DIOXIDE
                                                                                                    b) various NITROGEN OXIDES
2) When these _mix with clouds_ they form _acids_. This then falls as _acid rain_.
3) _Cars_ and _power stations_ are the _main causes_ of acid rain.

Acid Rain Kills Fish, Trees and Statues

1) Acid rain causes _lakes_ to become _acidic_ which has a _severe effect_ on its _ecosystem_.
2) The way this happens is that the acid causes _aluminium salts_ to _dissolve_ into the water. The resulting _aluminium ions_ are _poisonous_ to many _fish and birds_.
3) Acid rain kills _trees_.
4) Acid rain _damages limestone buildings_ and _ruins stone statues_.

Acid Rain is Prevented by Cleaning up Emissions

1) _Power stations_ now have _Acid Gas Scrubbers_ to take the harmful gases _out_ before they release their fumes into the atmosphere.
2) _Cars_ are now being fitted with _catalytic converters_ to clean up their _exhaust gases_.
3) The other way of reducing acid rain is simply to _reduce our usage_ of _fossil fuels_.

Catalytic converter

Learn about Acid Rain — and always take a coat...

There aren't too many details on acid rain. If you can't learn all this lot properly then you're just not trying. Don't forget they won't ask you easy stuff like "Is acid rain caused by cars or monkeys?", they'll test you on trickier stuff like "Which gases cause acid rain and why?". _Learn and enjoy._ And _smile_. ☺

SECTION FIVE — LIVING THINGS IN THEIR ENVIRONMENT   NEAB SYLLABUS

Problems Caused By Farming

Human Impact on the Environment

Farming Produces a Lot of Food, Which is Great but...

1) Farming is important to us because it allows us to produce *a lot of food* from *less and less land*.
2) These days it has become quite a *high-tech* industry. Food production is *big business*.
3) The great advantage of this is a *huge variety* of *top quality* foods, *all year round*, at *cheap prices*.
4) This is a far cry from Britain *50 years ago* when food had to be *rationed* by the government because there simply *wasn't enough* for everyone. That's hard to imagine today... but try...

Fertilisers Damage Lakes and Rivers — Eutrophication

1) *Fertilisers* which contain *nitrates* are essential to *modern farming*.
2) Without them crops wouldn't grow nearly so well, and *food yields* would be *well down*.
3) This is because the crops take *nitrates* out of the soil and these nitrates need to be *replaced*.
4) The *problems* start if some of the *rich fertiliser* finds its way into *rivers* and *streams*.
5) This happens quite easily if *too much fertiliser* is applied, especially if it rains soon afterwards.
6) The result is EUTROPHICATION, which basically means "*too much of a good thing*".
   (*Raw sewage* pumped into rivers also causes EUTROPHICATION by providing food for microbes.)

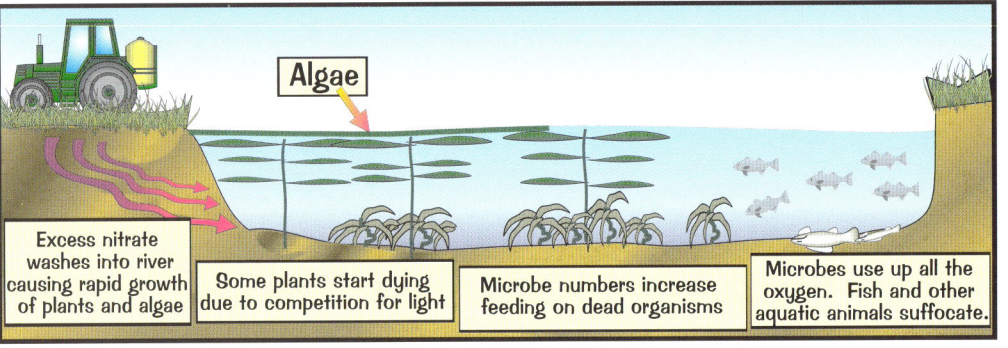

As the picture shows, *too many nitrates* in the water cause a sequence of "*mega-growth*", "*mega-death*" and "*mega-decay*" involving most of the *plant* and *animal life* in the water.

7) *Farmers* need to take *a lot more care* when spreading *artificial fertilisers*.

Deforestation increases CO_2 Levels and the Greenhouse Effect

We have already pretty well deforested OUR COUNTRY. Now many *under-developed* tropical countries are doing the same for timber and to provide land for agriculture. One of the main *environmental problems* this causes is an *increase* in the *greenhouse gas*, *carbon dioxide* (CO_2). Deforestation increases CO_2 in the atmosphere in two ways:

1) The trees unsuitable for timber are *burned* releasing CO_2 directly into the atmosphere.
   Microbes also release CO_2 by *decaying* the felled trees that remain.
2) Because living trees use CO_2 for *photosynthesis*, removing these trees means *less* CO_2 is removed from the atmosphere.

"There's nowt wrong wi' just spreadin' muck on it..."

Make sure you distinguish between *pesticides* (which kill bugs) and *fertilisers* (which supply nutrients to the plants). They can both cause harm but for totally different reasons. You have to learn the details carefully. *Mini-essay* time again I'd say. *Cover the page and scribble*...

NEAB Syllabus — SECTION FIVE — LIVING THINGS IN THEIR ENVIRONMENT

The Greenhouse Effect

Human Impact on the Environment

Carbon Dioxide and Methane Trap Heat from the Sun

1) The temperature of the Earth is a balance between the heat it gets from the Sun and the heat it radiates back out into space.
2) The atmosphere acts like an insulating layer and keeps some of the heat in.
3) This is exactly what happens in a greenhouse or a conservatory. The sun shines into it and the glass keeps the heat in so it just gets hotter and hotter.

4) There are several different gases in the atmosphere which are very good at keeping the heat in. They are called "greenhouse gases", oddly enough. The main ones that we worry about are methane and carbon dioxide, because the levels of these are slowly rising.
5) The Greenhouse Effect is causing the Earth to warm up very slowly.

The Greenhouse Effect may cause Flooding and Drought

1) An increase in the Earth's temperature of only a few degrees Celsius could cause big changes in weather patterns and climate which may lead to drought or flooding in certain areas.
2) Higher temperatures could melt the polar ice-caps which would raise sea-levels and could cause flooding to many low-lying coastal parts of the world including many major cities.

Modern Industrial Life is Causing the Greenhouse Effect

1) The level of CO_2 in the atmosphere used to be nicely balanced between the CO_2 released by respiration (of animals and plants) and the CO_2 absorbed by photosynthesis.
2) However, mankind has been burning massive amounts of fossil fuels in the last two hundred years or so.
3) We have also been cutting down trees all over the world to make space for living and farming. This is called deforestation.
4) The level of CO_2 in the atmosphere has gone up by about 20%, and will continue to rise ever more steeply as long as we keep burning fossil fuels — just look at that graph — eek!

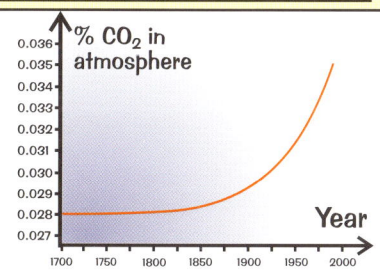

Methane is Also a Problem

1) Methane gas is also contributing to the Greenhouse Effect.
2) It's produced naturally from various sources, such as natural marshland.
3) However, the two sources of methane which are on the increase are:
   a) Rice growing
   b) Cattle rearing — it's the cows "pumping" that's the problem, believe it or not.

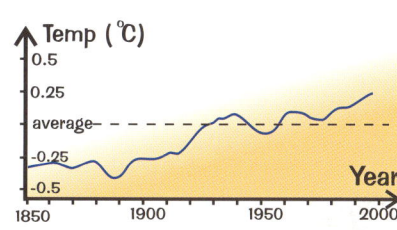

Learn the facts first — then start building your ark...

I bet you never realised there were so many drivelly details on the Greenhouse Effect. Well there *are* and I'm afraid they could all come up in your Exam, so you just gotta learn them. Use the good old mini-essay method for each section, and scribble down what you know...

SECTION FIVE — LIVING THINGS IN THEIR ENVIRONMENT NEAB SYLLABUS

Food Webs

Energy and Nutrient Transfer

A Woodland Food Web

Food webs are pretty easy really. Hideously easy in fact.

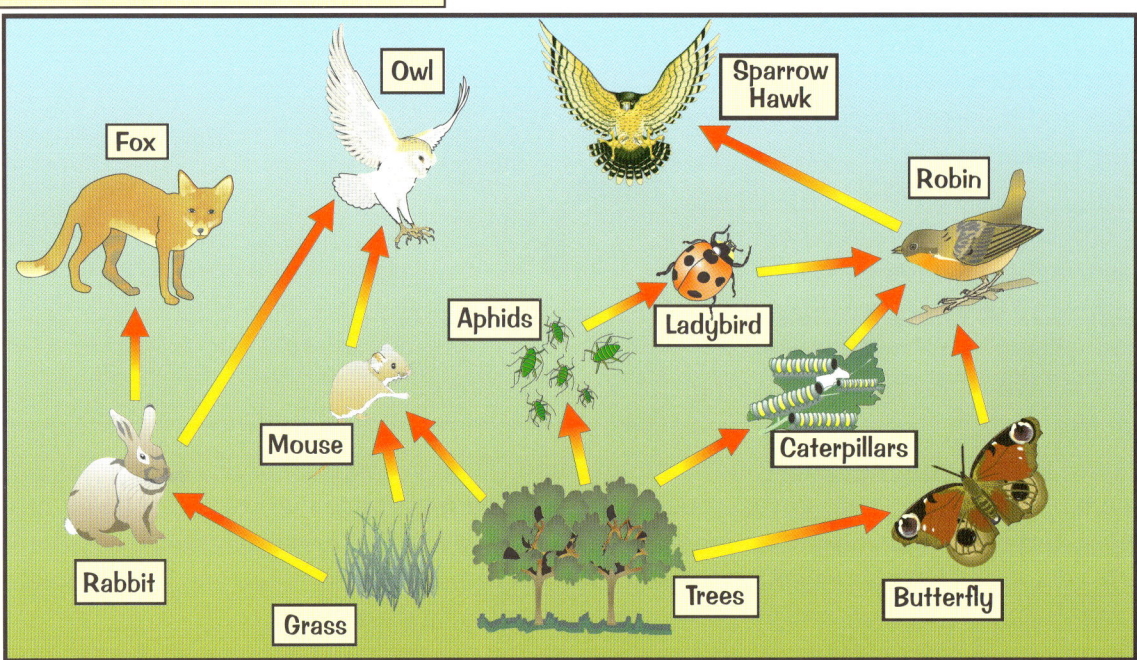

Food Chains — the Arrows show where the Energy goes

1) A _food chain_ is just part of a _food web_, starting at the bottom and _following the arrows_ up.
2) Remember, the _arrows_ show which way the _food energy travels_.
3) Don't mix up _who eats who_ either!
   The arrow means "_IS EATEN BY_", so you _follow the arrow_ to the one doing the _eating_.
4) From the woodland food web we could take this _food chain_:

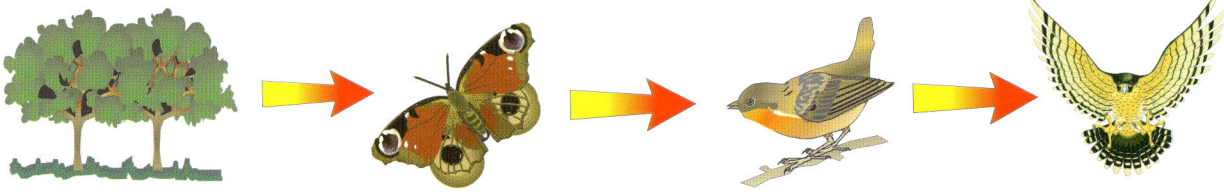

Terminology you need to know

1) **PRODUCER** — all _plants_ are _producers_. They use the Sun's energy to produce food energy.
2) **HERBIVORE** — animals which _only eat plants_, e.g. rabbits, caterpillars, aphids.
3) **CONSUMER** — all _animals_ are _consumers_. All _plants_ are _not_, because they are producers.
4) **PRIMARY CONSUMER** — animal which eats _producers_ (plants).
5) **SECONDARY CONSUMER** — animal which eats primary consumers.
6) **CARNIVORE** — eats _only animals_, never plants.
7) **TOP CARNIVORE** — is _not eaten by anything else_, except decomposers after it dies.
8) **OMNIVORE** — eats _both plants and animals_.
9) **DECOMPOSER** — lives off all _dead material_ — producers, consumers, top carnivore, the lot.

Learn about Food Webs, terminology and all...

That's got to be the prettiest food web ever drawn, wouldn't you say? Yeah well, anyway, the pretty pictures are the easy bit. It's those _9 definitions_ which you really need to work at. That's what'll sort out the sheep from the goats in the Exam. So make sure you _know them all_.

NEAB Syllabus — SECTION FIVE — LIVING THINGS IN THEIR ENVIRONMENT

Making Holes in Food Webs

Energy and Nutrient Transfer

A Typical Food Web for a Pond

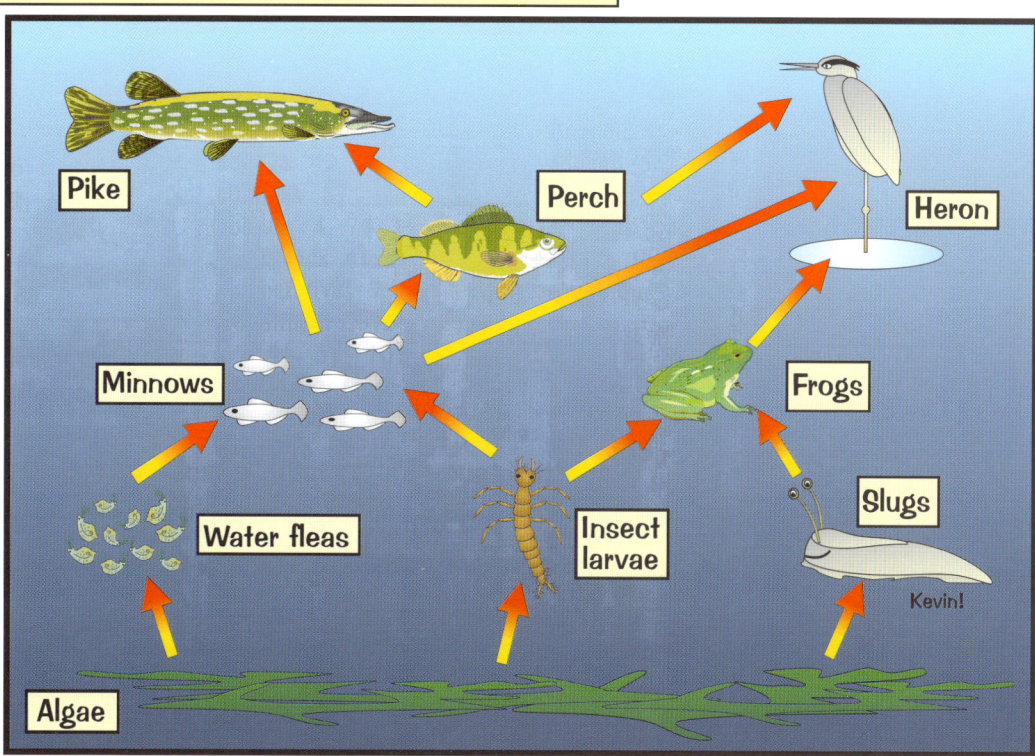

Exam Q. — What happens if you take out the frogs...?

1) This is the usual Exam question.
2) One of the animals is wiped out — what effect will this have on the other creatures?
3) For example, if all the frogs were removed what'd happen to the number of slugs or perch?
4) It's simple enough, but you do have to think it through fairly carefully:
   a) **SLUGS** would increase because there'd be nothing to eat them now.
   b) **PERCH** is a bit trickier. With no frogs the herons will get hungry and so will eat more perch (and minnows and insect larvae), so the perch will in fact decrease in number.

You just have to understand the diagrams (i.e. who eats who) and think about it real carefully. Think about which animals won't now get eaten, and which animals will go hungry, and work out what they'll do about it — and the effect that will have on all the other things in the web.

Another Exam Q. — What if you took out the Minnows...?

1) First of all, water fleas would increase.
2) Perch on the other hand would be really struggling. They'd get hungry for a start, but they'd also get eaten a lot more by pike and heron. Toughsky.
3) Frogs would initially benefit from more insect larvae all to themselves, but would then suffer from heron eating more frogs due to there being no minnows and fewer perch.
4) Slugs would therefore benefit because the frogs would be eating more insect larvae (instead of slugs) and also getting eaten by heron. It's all real simple if you just think it out.

Learn about making holes in Food webs...

If they give you a food web question you can bet your very last fruit cake they're gonna want to wipe out one of the creatures and ask you what happens then. Practise with both these food webs by wiping out organisms (only one at a time!) and deciding what'll happen to the others.

SECTION FIVE — LIVING THINGS IN THEIR ENVIRONMENT   **NEAB** SYLLABUS

Pyramids Of Number & Biomass

Energy and Nutrient Transfer

This is hideously easy too. Just _make sure you know_ what _all_ the pyramids mean.

Each _Level_ you go up, there's _fewer of them..._

_5000_ dandelions... feed.. _100_ rabbits... which feed.... _one_ fox.

IN OTHER WORDS, each time you go _up one level_ the _number of organisms goes down_ — _A LOT_.
It takes _a lot_ of food from the level _below_ to keep any one animal alive.
This gives us the good old _number pyramid_:

A typical pyramid of numbers

This is the _basic idea_ anyway. But there are cases where the pyramid is _not a pyramid at all_:

Number Pyramids Sometimes Look Wrong

This is a _pyramid_ except for the _top layer_ which goes _huge_:

500 Fleas
1 Fox
100 Rabbits
5,000 Dandelions

This is a _pyramid_ apart from the _bottom layer_ which is _way too small_:

1 Partridge
1000 Ladybirds
3,000 Aphids
1 Pear tree

Biomass Pyramids Never Look Wrong

When _number pyramids_ seem to go _wrong_ like this, then the good old PYRAMID OF BIOMASS comes to the rescue. _Biomass_ is just how much all the creatures at each level would "_weigh_" if you _put them all together_. So the _one pear tree_ would have a _big biomass_ and the _hundreds of fleas_ would have _a very small biomass_. Biomass pyramids are _ALWAYS the right shape_:

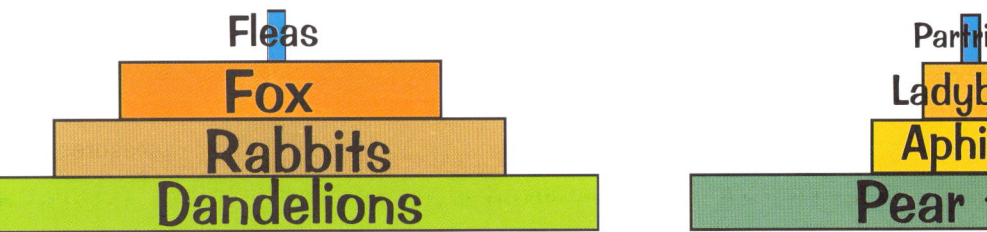

Basically, _biomass pyramids_ are the only _sensible_ way to do it — it's just that _number pyramids_ are _easier to understand_.

Now Children, get your coloured wooden blocks out...

...hideously easy...

Energy Transfer & Efficient Food

Energy and Nutrient Transfer

All that Energy just Disappears Somehow...

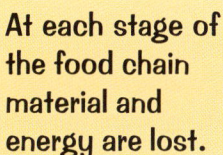

1) Energy from the <u>SUN</u> is the <u>source of energy</u> for <u>all life on Earth</u>.

2) <u>Plants</u> convert <u>a small %</u> of the light energy that falls on them <u>into glucose</u>. This <u>energy</u> then works its way through the <u>food web</u>.

3) The <u>ENERGY lost</u> at each stage is used for <u>staying alive</u>, i.e. in <u>respiration</u>, which powers <u>all life processes</u>, including <u>movement</u>.

At each stage of the food chain material and energy are lost.

This explains why you get <u>biomass pyramids</u>. Most of the biomass is lost and so does <u>not</u> become biomass in the <u>next level up</u>.

4) Most of this energy is eventually <u>lost to the surroundings</u> as <u>heat</u>. This is especially true for <u>mammals and birds</u> whose bodies must be kept at a <u>constant temperature</u> which is normally higher than their surroundings.

HEAT LOSS

MATERIALS LOST IN ANIMAL'S WASTE

5) <u>Material and energy</u> is also lost from the food chain in the <u>droppings</u> — they burn when dried, proving they still have chemical energy in them.

Try it next time you're camping — you'll find you enjoy your midnight sausages that much more when cooked over a blazing mound of dried sheep poo.

Two Ways to Improve the "Efficiency" of Food Production

1) Reducing the Number of Stages in Food Chains

1) <u>For a given area of land</u>, you can produce <u>a lot more food</u> (for humans) by growing <u>crops</u> rather than by <u>grazing animals</u>. This is because you are reducing the number of stages in the food chain. Only <u>10%</u> of what beef cattle eat becomes useful meat for people to eat.

2) However, don't forget that just eating <u>crops</u> can quickly lead to <u>malnutrition</u> through lack of essential <u>proteins</u> and <u>minerals</u>, unless a varied enough diet is achieved. Also remember that <u>some land is unsuitable for growing crops</u> like <u>moorland</u> or <u>fellsides</u>. In these places, animals like <u>sheep</u> and <u>deer</u> are often the <u>best</u> way to get food from the land.

2) Restricting the Energy Lost by Farm Animals

1) In 'civilised' countries such as ours, animals like <u>pigs</u> and <u>chickens</u> are reared in strict conditions of <u>limited movement</u> and <u>artificial warmth</u>, in order to reduce their <u>energy losses</u> to a minimum.

2) In other words keep them <u>still enough</u> and <u>hot enough</u> and they won't need <u>feeding as much</u>. It's as <u>simple</u> and as <u>horrible</u> as that. If you deny them even the simplest of simple pleasures in their short little stay on this planet before you eat them, then it won't cost you as much in feed. Lovely.

3) But <u>intensively reared</u> animals like chickens and pigs, kept in a little shed all their life, <u>still require land indirectly</u> because they still need <u>feeding</u>, so land is needed to <u>grow</u> their "feed" on.
So would it be <u>so terrible</u> to let them have a little corner of it in the sunshine somewhere, huh...?

Locked up in a little cage with no sunlight — who'd work in a bank...

Phew! Just look at all those words crammed onto one page. Geesh.... I mean blimey, it almost looks like a page from a normal science book. Almost. Anyway, there it all is, on the page, just waiting to be blended with the infinite void inside your head. <u>Learn and enjoy</u>... and <u>scribble</u>.

SECTION FIVE — LIVING THINGS IN THEIR ENVIRONMENT   *NEAB* SYLLABUS

Decomposition & the Carbon Cycle

Nutrient Cycles

Another sixties pop group? Sadly not.

1) <u>Living things</u> are made of <u>materials</u> they take from the world around them.
2) When they <u>decompose</u>, ashes are returned to ashes, and dust to dust, as it were.
3) In other words <u>the elements they contain</u> are returned to the <u>soil</u> where they came from <u>originally</u>.
4) These elements are then <u>used by plants</u> to grow and the whole cycle <u>repeats</u> over and over again.

Decomposition is carried out by Bacteria and Fungi

1) All <u>plant matter</u> and <u>dead animals</u> are broken down (digested) by <u>microbes</u>.
2) This happens everywhere in <u>nature</u>, and also in <u>compost heaps</u> and <u>sewage works</u>.
3) All the important <u>elements</u> are thus <u>recycled</u>:
   <u>Carbon</u>, <u>Hydrogen</u>, <u>Oxygen</u> and <u>Nitrogen</u>.
4) The <u>ideal conditions</u> for creating <u>compost</u> are:
   a) **WARMTH**
   b) **MOISTURE**
   c) **OXYGEN (AIR)**
   d) **MICROBES** (i.e. <u>bacteria</u> and <u>fungi</u>)
   e) **ORGANIC MATTER** cut into <u>small pieces</u>.
   Make sure you <u>learn them</u> — ALL FIVE.

There's a kid I know, and everyone calls him "the party mushroom". I'm not sure why really — they just say he's a fun guy to be with...

The Carbon Cycle Shows how Carbon is Recycled

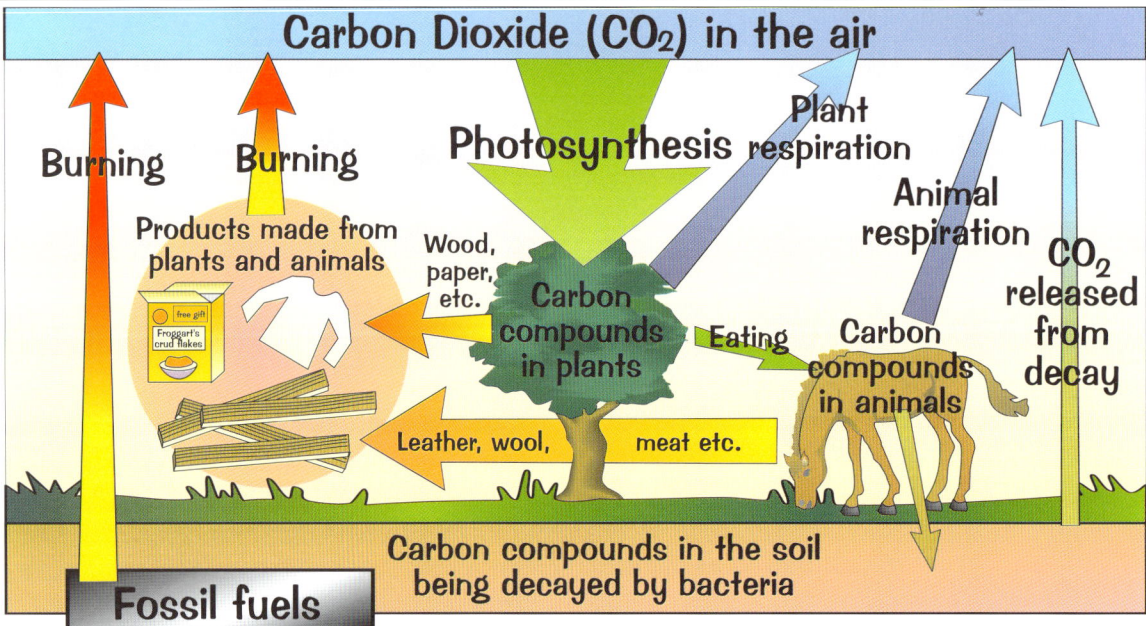

This diagram isn't half as bad as it looks. **LEARN** these important points:

1) There's only <u>one arrow</u> going <u>DOWN</u>. The whole thing is "powered" by <u>photosynthesis</u>.
2) Both plant and animal <u>respiration</u> puts CO_2 <u>back into the atmosphere</u>.
3) <u>Plants</u> convert the carbon in <u>CO_2 from the air</u> into <u>fats</u>, <u>carbohydrates</u> and <u>proteins</u>.
4) These can then go <u>three ways</u>: <u>be eaten</u>, <u>decay</u> or be turned into <u>useful products</u> by man.
5) <u>Eating</u> transfers some of the fats, proteins and carbohydrates to <u>new</u> fats, carbohydrates and proteins <u>in the animal</u> doing the eating.
6) Ultimately these plant and animal products either <u>decay</u> or are <u>burned</u> and <u>CO_2 is released</u>.

On Ilkley Moor ba 'tat, On Ilkley Moor ba 'tat... ♪ ...where the dogs play football ♪

Learn the five ideal conditions for compost making. They like asking about that.
Sketch out your <u>own simplified version</u> of the carbon cycle, making sure it contains all the labels.
Practise <u>scribbling</u> it out <u>from memory</u>. And <u>keep trying till you can</u>.

NEAB SYLLABUS — SECTION FIVE — LIVING THINGS IN THEIR ENVIRONMENT

The Nitrogen Cycle

Nutrient Cycles

The _constant cycling_ of nitrogen through the atmosphere, soil and living organisms is called the _nitrogen cycle_.

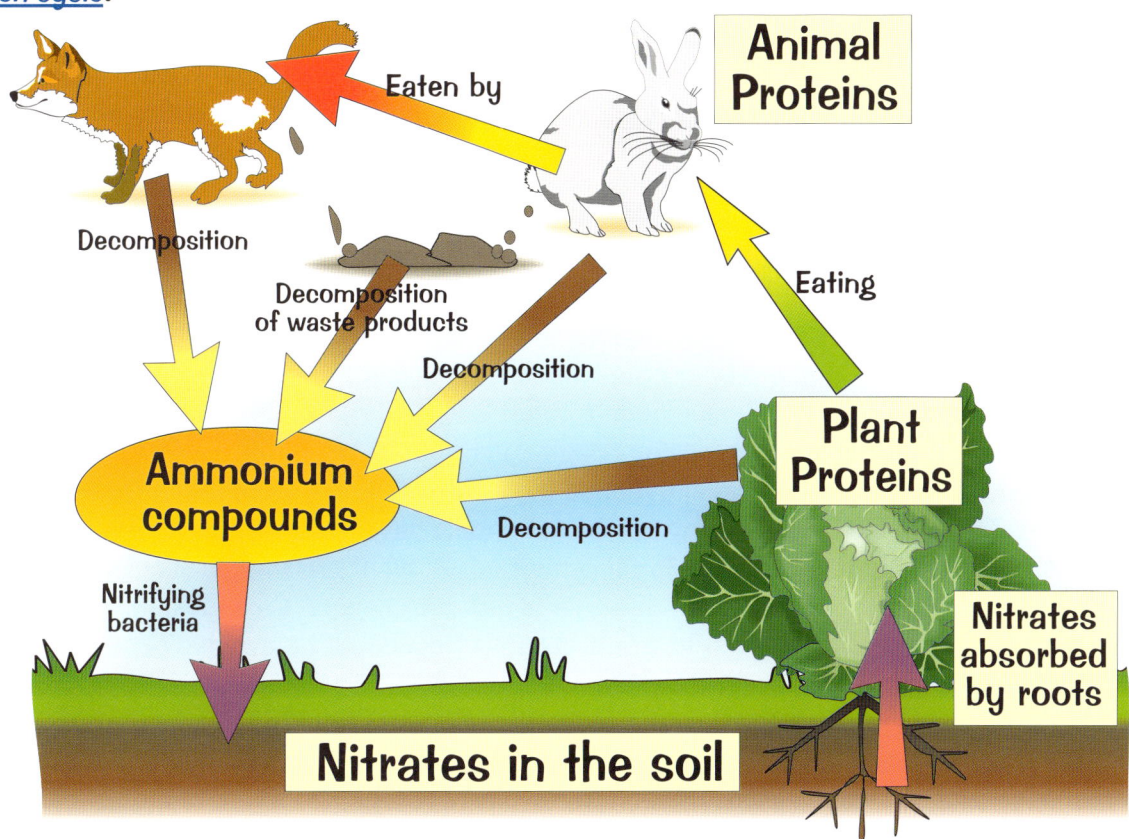

There are **Five** Simple Stages to Learn

1) _Green plants_ absorb nitrogen in the form of _nitrates_ from the soil. _Nitrogen_ is an _important element_ in making _proteins_ for plants and animals.

2) _Animals_ can't use nitrogen directly and so must therefore _eat the plants_ to obtain it. Of course other animals then eat these animals to get their nitrogen.

3) _Any organic waste_, i.e. rotting plants or dead animals or animal poo, is broken down by _microbes_ into _ammonium compounds_. By the time the microbes and other organisms that break down this decaying matter have finished, almost _all the energy_ originally captured by the green plants has been _recycled_. Organisms that do this decomposing job, such as the microbes, are called _detritus feeders_. Detritus is simply the name given to all the decaying matter.

4) _Nitrifying bacteria_ turn the _ammonium compounds_ produced by the microbes into _useful nitrates_.

5) These _nitrates_ can then once more be absorbed by the roots of _green plants_.

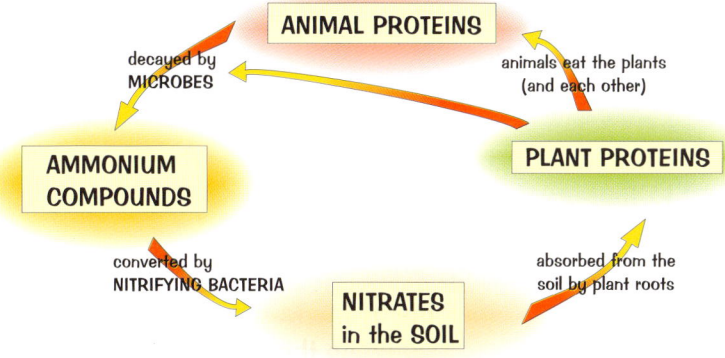

By Gum, you young 'uns have some stuff to learn...

It's really "grisly grimsdike" is the Nitrogen Cycle, I think. But the fun guys at the Exam Board want you to know all about it, so there you go. _Have a good time... and smile!_ ☺

SECTION FIVE — LIVING THINGS IN THEIR ENVIRONMENT   NEAB SYLLABUS

Revision Summary for Section Five

There's a lot of words in Section Five. Most topics are pretty waffly with a lot of drivelly facts, and it can be real hard to learn them all. But learn them you must. You need to practise scribbling down what you can remember on each topic, and then checking back to see what you missed. These questions give you a pretty good idea of what you should know. You need to practise and practise them — till you can float through them all, like a cloud or something.

1) Name the four factors that affect individual organisms on a daily basis.
2) What are the *five* basic things which determine the size of a population of a species?
3) List seven survival features of the polar bear and of the camel. List five survival features for the cactus.
4) Give five survival features for the lion and for the rabbit.
5) Sketch a graph of prey and predator populations and explain the shapes.
6) What is happening to the world population? What is largely responsible for this trend?
7) What problems does a rapidly increasing population create for a country?
8) What are the four main ways humans reduce the land available for other plants and animals.
9) What effect does the ever-increasing number of people have on the environment?
10) What is the great bonus of modern farming methods? What are the drawbacks?
11) What happens when too much nitrate fertiliser is put onto fields? Give full details.
12) What is the big fancy name given to this problem? How can it be avoided?
13) How does deforestation affect the climate?
14) Which two gases are the biggest cause of the greenhouse effect?
15) Explain how the greenhouse effect happens. What dire consequences could there be?
16) What is causing the rise in levels of each the two problem gases. What is the solution?
17) Which gases cause acid rain? Where do these gases come from?
18) What are the three main harmful effects of acid rain? Explain exactly how fish are killed.
19) Give three ways that acid rain can be reduced.
20) What are the three main sources of atmospheric pollution?
21) What are the precise environmental effects of each of these three sources of pollution?
22) Describe what food chains and food webs are. Give two examples of both.
23) Write down the 9 technical terms for food webs (P.86) and give a definition of each one.
24) What is the basic approach to questions which make holes in food webs?
25) What are number pyramids? Why do you generally get a pyramid of numbers?
26) Why do number pyramids sometimes go wrong, and which pyramids are always right?
27) Where does the energy in a food chain originate? What happens to the energy?
28) How much energy and biomass pass from one trophic level to the next?
29) Where does the rest go? What does this mean for farming methods where food is scarce?
30) How is this idea used to cut costs in rearing pigs and chickens in this country? Is it nice?
31) Which two organisms are responsible for the decay of organic matter?
32) What are the five ideal conditions for making compost? Draw a compost maker.
33) What is the Carbon Cycle all to do with? Copy and fill in as much of it from memory as you can.

34) What is the Nitrogen Cycle all about? Draw as much of it from memory as you can.
35) What do the four types of bacteria in the Nitrogen Cycle actually do?

NEAB Syllabus   SECTION FIVE — LIVING THINGS IN THEIR ENVIRONMENT

Index

A
a nice life 36
a real effort 74
a veritable dream 73
absorbed 10
acid gas scrubbers 79
acid rain 79
active uptake 8, 31, 42
addictive 36
ADH 24, 28, 31
adrenal gland 24
adrenaline 24
aerobic respiration 20
air movement 46
alcohol 37
allele 53, 60, 62, 65
alveoli 6, 18, 19
always take a coat 79
amber 71
amino acids 11, 30, 42, 43, 55
amylase 11
anaerobic respiration 20
anchorage 39
animal cells 1
animal characteristics 51
animal poo 87
another jolly page 23
anti diuretic hormone.
    See ADH
antibiotics 36
antibodies 17, 34
antitoxins 17, 34
anus 10
aorta 13, 14, 15
aphids 82
arctic creatures 76
arteries 13, 14, 15, 16
artificial fertilisers 80
artificial selection 64
artificially inseminated 66
atmosphere 86
atrium 14, 15
auxins 44
axon 23

B
backflow 14
background radiation 58
bacteria 10, 17, 32, 54, 68, 86
barrier against microbes 33
big ears 72, 77
big fancy words 52, 74
big molecules 6, 11
big pink sponges 18
big problems 78
big surface area 4, 8, 11, 39, 40, 47
big-eared rabbits 72
bile 10, 11
biomass pyramids 84
birth rate 78
bladder 30, 31
block diagram of a reflex arc 23
blood 16, 17, 30, 31
blood clots 17, 33
blood plasma 24, 28
blood sugar 24, 25, 28
blood supply 29
blood vessels 13, 16, 36
blue budgies 58
body cells 19
body temperature 28, 29, 76
bogs 71
brain 22, 29, 31
breathing 18, 30
breathing rate 24
breeding 64
bronchi 18
bronchiole 18, 19
bronchitis 36
bronchus 18
bulls 66
burst 7

C
calcium 12
camel 76
camouflage 77
cancer 58
capillaries 13, 16, 19, 28
carbohydrase 10, 11
carbohydrate foods 25
carbohydrates 12
carbon dioxide 5, 19, 28, 40, 41, 79, 81, 86
carcinogens 58
carnivore 82
carrier 62
carrot plants 42
cars 79
cat 50
catalysts 11
catalytic converters 79
caterpillars 82
cattle rearing 81
ceaning up emissions 78
cell division 54
cell elongation process 44
cell fibres 54
cell membrane 1, 6
cell nucleus 52, 53
cell sap 1
cell wall 1, 7, 42
cells 1, 42
cellulose 1, 42
central nervous system 22
characteristics 58, 61, 64
checkerboard 59
cheeky bee 23
chemical messengers 24
chemical stimuli 22
chemicals 23, 58
chlorophyll 1, 41
chloroplasts 1, 2, 40
chromosomes 52-57, 59
cigarette smoke 58
cilia 33, 36
ciliary muscles 21
circulatory system 13
clones 45, 54, 66
clot 17
cockroach 73
common sense 77
competition 75
compost heaps 86
concentration 5, 6, 7
concentration gradient 8
connector neuron 23
constant internal environment 28
consumer 82
contaminated food 33
contraception 78
contraceptive pill 27
cooking oil 42
copious blood supply 6, 19
crazy acrobatics 61
crazy cross-breed 65
cross-breeding 61
cuttings 45, 67
cycle 26
cystic fibrosis 62
cytoplasm 1, 9

D
daffodils 54
dandelions 84
Darwin's theory 72
daughter cells 54
dead cert 40
dead plants or animals 69
dead spots 43
death 36
death rate 78
decay microbes 71
decomposer 82
decomposition 86
defences 33
deficiency symptoms 43
deforestation 81
delightful name 52
dendron 23
deoxygenated blood 13, 14, 16
desert creatures 76
diabetes 25, 68
dialysis tubing 7
diaphragm 18
diet 12
dietary fibre 12
diffusion 5, 6, 7, 19
digestive enzymes 11
digestive system 3, 10, 32
dinky little ears 76
dinosaurs 69
dirty water 33
disease 17, 32-34, 66, 75
disease-resistance 64
DNA 32, 52-55, 68
dominant 52, 60-63
double circulatory system 13
double helix 52
double pump 14
drivelly facts 88
droop 47
drought 81
drugs 36, 68

Index

E
ears 22
easy peasy 24
ecosystem 79
eeek 39
effector 22
effects of environment 51
efficient food 85
egg cells 2, 26, 52, 56
egg production 24
elastic 16
electrical impulses 22, 23
electrical signal 23
EM spectrum 58
embryo transplants in
    cows 66
emissions 78
emphysema 36
emulsifies fats 11
energy 20, 42
energy transfer 85
environment 69
environmental damage 78
environmental
    problems 80
environmental variation 50
enzymes 3, 10, 11,
    29, 41, 43, 68
epiglottis 18
equation 20, 40
eutrophication 80
evaporation 46
every cell in the body 13
evolution 58, 69, 73
exchange surface 6, 19
exercise 20, 25
exhaust gases 79
extinction 69
extra hair 24
eyes 21, 22

F
F1, F2 generations 60, 61
faeces 10
fancy words 5, 28, 61
fantastic 36
farming 80
fast-moving creatures 13
fateful and magical
    moment 52
fats 10, 11, 12
fatty acids/glycerol 11

fellsides 85
female menstrual cycle 26
fertilisation 59
fertilised egg 26
fertiliser 43
fertility treatment 27
fight or flight reaction 24
filters 30
fingers 28
fish 13
fish, trees and statues 79
fitness and the
    oxygen debt 20
flaccid 2, 47
fleas 33, 84
flooding 81
flower 39
flu and colds 35
fluoride 12
flying doughnut 16
focusing 21
follicle stimulating
    hormone. *See* FSH
fond farewell 10
food 10, 12, 13,
    20, 30, 40
food chains 82
food energy 82
food for thought 12
food growing business 45
food webs 82
fossil fuels 79, 81
fossils 69, 70
foxes 77, 84
frogs 83
fruits 42, 45
FSH 24, 27
full of pips! 45
fun guy 86, 87
fungi 86

G
gall bladder 10
gametes 52, 56, 57,
    59, 61, 63
gas exchange 19
gene 52, 53, 60, 68
gene pool 65
gene types 59, 61, 62, 63
genes 50, 55, 56, 72
genetic diseases 63

genetic inheritance
    diagram 62
genetic variation 50
genetics 52
get your head round it 74
girl or boy? 59
glaciers 71
glands 22, 24
glandular tissue 3
glucagon 25
glucose 6, 7, 20,
    25, 31, 40, 42
gobble up 17
good clean fun 23
goodness knows 13
gory diagrams 37
Grand Canyon 71
gravity 44
grazers 75
green light 41
green plants 40
greenhouse effect 81
greenhouses 41
grisly bits and bobs 38
grisly grimsdike 87
grisly stuff 33
growth hormones 44,
    45, 68
guard cells 2, 7, 40, 47
gullet 10
gut 25

H
haemoglobin 2, 12, 16, 55
hairs 29
hairy mammoth 69, 71
hamsters 61
haploid gametes 56
health inspectors 73
healthy growth 43
heart 13, 14
heart attacks and strokes 36
heart rate 24
heart valves 14
heat 28, 85
herbivore 82
herons 83
heterozygous 52, 60, 61
hideously easy 82, 84
high concentration 5, 6
high pressure 13, 16

high-tech farming 66, 67
holes in food webs 83
homeostasis 28
homologous 57
homologous pairs 56
homozygous 52, 60, 61
hoof 69
hormones 24, 25, 27,
    28, 44, 66
horse 69
huffing and puffing 18
human chromosomes 57
humidity 46
hump 76
Huntington's chorea 63
hydrochloric acid 10, 33
hydrogen 86

I
identical twins 50, 66
Ilkley Moor 86
immune system 34
immunisation 35
implanted 66
infinite glory 10
infinite void 85
insulin 24, 25, 68
intensively reared
    animals 85
intestine 10
ions 28, 30, 31, 39
iris 21
iron 12, 16
it makes your head
    hurt 58
it's a nice trick if you can
    do it 37
it's all clever stuff 8
it's real tricky 27

J
jugular vein 13

K
keratin 55
kidneys 28, 30, 31
killing weeds 45
kind of clever 6

L
lactic acid 20
lakes and rivers 80
large chunk 1

Index

large intestine 10
large surface area 76
larynx 18
leaf structure 47
leaves 39, 40, 42, 46
lens (the eye) 21
LH 24
life processes 1, 85
life's full of little mysteries 13
life's tough 74
light and photosynthesis 41
light receptors 21, 23
light sensitive 21
lignin 48
like a cloud or something 88
limiting factor 41
lion 77
lipase 10, 11
lipids 42
liver 10, 12, 28, 30
low concentration 5, 6
low pressure 13
lumen 16
lung cancer 36
lungs 13, 18, 19, 28
luteinising hormone. See LH

M

malaria 33, 63
male or female 59
malnutrition 85
margarine 42
mega-death 80
meiosis 56, 57
melting of the polar ice-caps 81
menstrual cycle 26
metabolism 25, 29
methane 81
microbes 17, 32, 34
middle toe 69
midnight sausages 85
minerals 3, 8, 12, 42, 43, 46, 48
minnows 83
missing links 69
mitosis 52, 54, 55

modern farming 64, 80
modern farming methods 78
moist lining 6, 19
monoculture 43
monohybrid crosses 61
moorland 85
mosquitos 33, 68
motor neurons 22, 23
MRS NERG 1
mucus 3, 33, 62
multiple births 26
murdered 71
muscles 14, 22, 28
muscular tissue 3
mutagens 58
mutations 58, 72

N

natural immunity 35
natural selection 58, 72, 73
near and distant objects 21
nerve cells 22
nerve fibres 22
nerve impulses 23, 28
nerves 12, 24
nervous impulses 29
nervous system 22
neurons 22, 23
nicotine 36
nitrates 42, 43, 80, 86
nitrogen cycle 87
nitrogen oxides 79
nose 22
not even remotely scary 56
nuclear radiation 58
nucleus 1, 32, 53, 54, 57
number pyramid 84
nutrients 43
nutrition 12

O

oesophagus 10
oestrogen 24
offspring 59
olden times 65
omnivore 82
organic matter 86
organic waste 87
organs 28
osmosis 7, 42, 47
outward characteristics 57
ovaries 24, 26, 56

oxygen 5, 13, 19, 20, 40, 86
oxygen debt 20
oxygenated blood 13, 14, 16
oxyhaemoglobin 16, 19

P

pain receptor 23
palisade leaf cells 2, 40
pancreas 10, 24, 25, 28
partially permeable membrane 7
pear tree 84
pedigree dogs 65
penicillin 36
perch 83
perfect candidate 31
perfect eyebrows 50
perforated end-plates 48
perils of monoculture 43
petrification 70
pH 10
phloem Tubes 48
phosphates 43
photosynthesis 1, 2, 5, 39, 40, 41, 43, 86
physical activity 25
physical types 59, 61, 62, 63
pike 83
pips 45
pituitary gland 24, 28, 31
plant cells 1
plant hormones 44, 45
plants 39, 42, 46, 86
plasma 16
platelets 17
pleural fluid 18
poisonous 30, 36, 79
poisons 34
polar bear 76
polar ice-caps 81
pollen 39
pollinate 39, 45
poor growth 43
pores 47
potassium 43
potato 42, 54, 66
potato tubes 7
power stations 79

predator 75, 77
pressure 22
pretty serious stuff 74
pretty tough 38
prey 77
primary consumer 82
prizes! 38
producer 82
protease 10, 11
proteins 6, 11, 12, 42, 43, 55, 87
puberty 24
pummels 10
pump 14
pumping cycle 15
pupil 21
pyramids 84

Q

quick absorption 4

R

rabbits 77, 82, 84
radiation 58
rat flea 35
rate of photosynthesis 41
raw sewage 80
reabsorption 30
receptors 22
recessive genes 52, 60-63
rectum 10
red blood cells 16, 63
red meat 12
reflex arc 23
reflexes 22, 23
relay neuron 23
reproduce 66, 72
reproduction 54
reproductive cells 57
reproductive organs 56
resistant "strain" of bacteria 58
respiration 20, 42, 43, 85, 86
respiratory tract 33
responses 23
retina 21
rib muscles 18
ribcage 18
rice growing 81
ripening hormone, fruit 45
rock and soil strata 70

Index

roll off the tongue 61
root hair cell 4
root hairs 8, 39
rooting compound 45
roots 39, 43, 48
roughage 12
Rudyard Kipling 72

S
salivary amylase 10
salivary gands 10
salty meal 31
scrubbers 79
sea-levels 81
secondary consumer 82
secondary sexual
 characteristics 24
seedless grapes 45
seeds 42, 45
selective breeding 64
sense organs 22
sensitive 22
sensory neurons 22, 23
serious learning 45
severe downward
 spiral 36
sewage works 86
sexual characteristics 24
sexual intercourse 33
sexual reproduction 57
sheep 1
shivering 28
shoot tips 48
shoots and roots 44
shrivelling up like
 a prune 12
sickle cell anaemia 63
silly names 11, 16
simple sugars 11
skin 22, 28
slugs 83
small intestine 4, 10
small molecules 6
smaller molecules 11
smell 22
so there you go 87
sodium 12, 31
soil 39, 42, 43, 46
soil strata 70
solvents 36
some tough questions 9
sound-receptors 22
spectacularly dumb 9
sperm 2, 66
sperm cells 52, 56
sperm production 24
sphincters 10, 15, 30
spinal chord 22
spreadin' muck on it 80
starch 6, 11, 42, 48
statues 79
stem 39
sternum 18
stimuli, stimulus 22
stomach 10, 33
stomata 2, 5
storage organs 48
strain of bacteria or virus 35
strawberry 54, 66
strokes 36
strong and stiff 3, 48
stubborn cats
 notwithstanding 51
stunted growth 43
stupefyingly easy 69
sucrose 42
suffer 35
sugar 25, 31
sugar content 28
sugar solution 7
sugars 11
sulphur dioxide 79
Sun 81
sunlight 40
Sun's energy 82
sunshine 85
surface area 4, 6, 8, 10,
 19, 39, 40, 47, 76
survival of the fittest 72
sweat 30
sweat gland 29
sweating 76
swollen roots 42
symptoms 62
synapse 23

T
take out the frogs 83
taking the mickey 31
tar 36
target cells 24
taste 22
teeth and bones 12
temperature 28, 41
testes 24, 56
testosterone 24
the black death 33
the Pill 27
there's no drivel 22
thermoregulatory centre 29
thorax 18
tips 44
tissue fluid 28
tongue 22
too cold 29
too hot 29
too many people 78
too much of a good thing 80
top carnivore 82
touch 22
toxins 17, 32, 34
trachea 18
transduce 22
transpiration 5, 46
transport 42, 48
turgid 2, 7, 47
turgor pressure 47
twins 50

U
ultra-violet light 58
upbringing 50
urea 28, 30, 31
ureter 30, 31
urine 30, 31
uterus lining 26

V
vacuole 1
valves 14, 16
variation in plants and
 animals 50
vectors 33
vegan 73
veins 13, 16, 30
ventricles 14, 15
very ill indeed 35
vigorous exercise 20, 25
villi 4, 10
viruses 32
visible light spectrum 41
visking tubing 7
vitamins 12
voice box 18

W
waste product 30
wastes 28, 31
water 3, 12, 31,
 40, 46, 48
water content 28, 30, 31
water fleas 83
water loss 76
water vapour 5
waxy layer 46
weedkillers 45
weeds 45
weird smell 5
what poetry 52
white blood cells 17, 34
wind pipe 18
winter 42
womb 26
wound 17
wreck your life 36

X
xylem tubes 3, 48

Y
yield 43, 64, 80
you gotta be pretty keen 27
you young 'uns have some
 stuff to learn 87
you're on your own, pal 35

Z
zygotes 52, 59, 61-63